The Book of Bipolar
According to Veronica

BY VERONICA MAY

Copyright © 2025 by Veronica May.

All rights reserved. No part of this publication may be reproduced, distributed, or transmitted in any form or by any means, including photocopying, recording, or other electronic or mechanical methods, without the prior written permission of the publisher, except in the case of brief quotations embodied in critical reviews and certain other noncommercial uses permitted by copyright law. For permission requests, contact the publisher at the website address below.

Author: Veronica May
Website: veronicamay.com
Publisher: Veronica May

The Book of Bipolar According to Veronica. First edition.

The recommendations, opinions, experiences, observations, or other information contained herein is provided "as is" and neither the author nor publisher make any representations or warranties of any kind, express or implied, about the accuracy, suitability, reliability, or completeness of this book's content. Any reliance a reader places on such information is therefore strictly at their own risk. All recommendations are made without guarantee on the part of the author and publisher. All the events herein are true to the best of the author's memory. To the maximum extent permitted by law, the author and publisher disclaim all liability from this publication's use. In no event will either author or publisher be liable to any reader for any loss or damage whatsoever arising from the use of the information contained in this book. This book is not a substitute for professional services, and readers are advised to seek professional aid in the event of emergency.

ISBN: 979-8-9924807-0-2

Acknowledgements and dedications

Thank you, to all the editors and beta readers of this book. The very first editors of this book went through a lot as it started with over 500 pages over a decade ago — the first editor being Kristine Rysberg. Thank you for seeing the mess and being a part of it. Then came Sharisse Coulter and Will Byrne with several rounds of edits and many useful notes. Sharisse, thank you for being the author that kept me writing. There were so many times I wanted to give up and you encouraged me through not only editing but words of wisdom from your experiences. Next up and final editor and all around great human, Amy Collette. You made the last part of this process feel pretty painless and for that I am relieved. Many others were involved in this process of editing.

There are too many folks here to thank. The Lindsays and Christines of the world. To all my former partners and to my current partner, I love you. Thank you for being with me. The friends and the family that say, "No, Veronica, we will not let you fall all the way." Thank you. Thank you. Thank you. Without you I truly wouldn't have made it long enough to finish his book. Having community to a person with a severe mental illness is life or death.

Above all, this book is dedicated to you, the reader. To you, the listener of my story. Whether you're reading this wondering if you might have bipolar or if you are a loved one questioning that for someone in your life. Whether you are a scholar in search of education or a mental health advocate looking for perspective. Welcome. I tried making chapters short and digestible so you can pick up and put down the book at your leisure.

I love you, Mom. I miss you, Dad. Thanks for taking the time to create me so I could create this.

That we all may take our difficult parts and show them to the world. "Love them or they will grow stronger," as my dear friend Meghan once said. One person can make a difference. I hope to always believe in this.

Table of Contents

Acknowledgements and dedications	iii
Meet the People in This Book	vii
Foreword by Lindsay	xiii
1 // Genesis	1
2 // Back to School	3
3 // The South Side of Mania	7
4 // Meet Alex	13
5 // The Alley Next to Target	15
6 // Finding the Lost	19
7 // Nun the Wiser	23
8 // Veronica Is Gone	25
9 // Way to Go, Noelle	31
10 // Go to Hell, North Unit	35
11 // Relax, It's Only Toilet Water	43
12 // Keep It on the Down Lo Mein	45
13 // Laughter Is Medicine	47
14 // Dr. Seek and Mr. Hide	49
15 // Sisters	51
16 // Shocking: It Still happens?	55
17 // Nice…Flower?	57
18 // Tables Turned	59
19 // Dentist Chair Bed, Please	61
20 // Do Better	65
21 // Going to Heaven: The Open Unit	67
22 // I Shall Be Released	71
23 // Psychiatwists and Turns	75
24 // The Difference in a Year	79
25 // Meet Lindsay	81
26 // Going Back for Seconds	83
27 // Emergency Shmergency	95
28 // Piano: A Grand Thing to Waste	101
29 // Sometimes You Get Punched	105
30 // The Virgin Veronica	107
31 // The Shot Heard Round the Hospital	109
32 // Staff? Hello?	115

33 // Visitation Vignette	117	52 // Burning Man	209
34 // If I Could Turn Back Time	121	53 // Weirdest. Surgery. Ever.	221
35 // Coming Up for Air	129	54 // Push Push Swipe	225
36 // O Brother, Where Art I?	131	55 // Small World	231
		56 // Meet the ICU Crew	233
37 // Camera One, Camera Two	133	57 // Music: The Real Hero	237
		58 // Why Don't You Cry about It?	241
38 // Take Me to Church	137		
39 // The Med Game	139	59 // Coming Alive Again	245
40 // We're All Just Cakes	141	60 // Sorry I'm Acting Like a Dick	247
41 // For Better or Worse, Repeat	143		
		61 // The Sunrays	251
42 // Real Joy	147	62 // "Agitated"	253
43 // Mom, Dad, I'm Gay…and Cray	151	63 // Hope Rings True	257
		64 // Hide AND Seek	259
44 // The Plan	153	65 // Teacher Becomes Student	261
45 // Impact of Me	159		
46 // Third Times a Charm	161	66 // The Plan, Analyzed	265
47 // Not ALL Bad	167	67 // My Progress	271
48 // Sage Advice	175	68 // The Interview I Didn't Get	273
49 // Water You Thinking About	181		
		69 // Until Next Time	275
50 // Hoo Ordered the Owl?	191	70 // Letter to Me	277
		Glossary	285
51 // Imposter Jesus	195		

Meet the People in This Book

Persons with Mental Illness

Veronica: Musician, music therapist, mental health advocate, and the author of this book. There are two of her:

> Lucid Veronica: Someone who can hold a job and support friends and family. A musician through and through. An illustrator and all-around good gal. Well-equipped with a joke or play on words. Warning: This book contains humor. Consult a doctor before reading. May die laughing.
>
> *Manic Veronica: An unpredictable woman. Sometimes elated, sometimes terrified, always in another world. And in the case of this book, Manic Veronica's voice will be the only writing in italics.*

Alex: The only person at the time that I knew with Bipolar I.

Mental Health Team

Dr. R: She is my go-to person when in crisis, and in my day-to-day life. She was the psychologist onsite at my first episode and had been my therapist from 2008 to 2021 until she stopped practicing privately. I saw her once a week and after years; we saw each other once or twice a month, depending on how I was doing. She is still one of my most valuable assets.

Dr. E: He was the psychiatrist onsite in my second hospital stay, and I kept him. He showed me the hope I didn't think existed in what he refers to as, "the art of psychiatry." Also, he never rushed through our appointments and asked me life questions—not just medication questions. Thankfully, he was my psychiatrist for nine years until he left psychiatry to dive into his painting passion.

Caretakers

Lindsay: My partner of three years who was with me during my second manic episode, my music duo partner of six years, and now, my friend who I know can't help but have my back for the last fifteen years and counting. And if the going were to ever get so tough for her, she would know I would never abandon her. She was a crucial part in my second and third episodes. She is a crucial part now, even though we live states apart. Lindsay is one of two lighthouses I somehow am able to find in the midst of a mental health storm. She now has a wife who is her lighthouse, with their daughter being the water of life around them, who they keep their lights on for now.

Christine: Lighthouse number two (in no particular order, so no fighting over who is number one lighthouse, you two). When I was delusional, when I had completely "lost my marbles," I had believed Christine was John the Baptist. Every time I am in full-blown mania, she becomes my disciple in the moments I am believing I am Jesus. When I read the bible as a kid, to me, John the Baptist was Jesus' most loyal, unwavering, consistent friend. That's Christine for you. Just like Lindsay, we will weather each other's storms. They have weathered many of mine. They love me in a way not everyone gets to experience. Christine is part of what we used to call "The Core." It consisted of three friends I made when I first moved to San Diego—Janet and Molly being the other two. That little group of women is now about twenty-five people strong these days. A network. A family. Christine knew me before my first break. She was my band manager for some years and has played a crucial role in all three of my episodes.

Noelle: My partner during the first episode who really broke ground with me in terms of understanding the beginning of a diagnosis. She also happened to be hanging out with me minutes after my second and third manic episodes broke. My first guide into the unknown. She truly took care of me in a way that may have felt long term, as my first episode took the longest to recover from. She's an activist and a musician. A healer of the communities she is a part of. A nurturer of the planet we live on.

Stephanie: My oldest sister, who took care of me during recovery for two of my episodes. My sister and I have a cord between us. The day it is cut by death will be something that changes the one who is still alive. She has saved my life more than once, and I'm not sure she's aware of that. From birth, Steph was told to "look after Veronica. Look after your younger sister." She maintains that role today. The day I get to help my sister will be a day I remember.

Mom: She stayed with me post-hospitalization for manic episode one. Mom and I have a special connection: music. We think alike and if I had a dollar for every time we've heard the other say "I was JUST thinking that!" I'd have enough dollars to buy groceries weekly at Whole Foods. We might disagree on some things, but these days she lets me be non-Catholic and I'm learning to let her be Catholic. I get my humor directly from this woman, however, when it comes to the best pun of all, Mum's the Queen. She and my stepdad, Gary, also visited the night before my second break.

Krista: My older sister who took care of me during my first manic episode. Krista and I met each other when we were around four years old. While by definition she and Brandon (brother) are my stepsiblings, I've always felt the love of family between all seven of us kids. She is just six months older than me, though if you meet her, she'll try to convince you she's the youngest. I have proof that I am the younger of the two, and if it comes to whipping out our birth certificates, I'm prepared. Krista and I are kindred spirits, and when we get to laughing, don't you dare try to stop us because we won't. I like to think I let Krista's goofy side out. I'm lucky to have three sisters I would go to the greatest lengths for.

Brandon: My brother who took care of me after my second manic episode. Brandon is one of my older brothers. I only grew up with two of the three brothers. Growing up, Brandon let me play catch with him while the girls played Barbies. He was faster, smarter, stronger, and I admired him more than he knows. He let me learn from him in ways he may not have seen.

Toby: A friend who was with me the night before my third manic episode. I still consider Toby a dear friend, but our season of friendship was short as she moved and I moved. We were both music therapists at the time. I believe every singing voice is beautiful, because it is our voice. I think if I had to listen to one singing voice for the rest of my life, it might be Toby's.

Becca: My partner in San Diego at the time of my third manic episode. The relationship was so new that Becca was left in the dark for a lot of my hospitalization. To say the least, I took Becca on a bumpy ride that landed us in Colorado where we both reside to this day, but in separate homes with new partners.

And, of course, Molly, Kristen, Allegra, Nikki, Janet, Jeffrey Joe, Michele, and the other many many supporters who were interviewed and a part of the story. Thank you, I love you.

Foreword by Lindsay

I fell bonkers in love with Veronica May from the moment I laid eyes (and ears) on her. She was so talented it made my stomach hurt and was so funny it made my cheeks hurt. She was so charismatic it made my lady parts hurt. To make a very long and complicated story short, V and I dated for three years and played music together as The Lovebirds for six years. As you'll soon learn in the following pages, we went through a lot together. A. Lot. In that time, I learned so much. She should probably create a diploma for me in Microsoft Paint or something.

I never really thought about mental health or mental illness until I met V. Looking back, this seems strange because I definitely struggled with anxiety, depression, and emotional and binge eating from a very young age. But in my mind, these were embarrassing personal problems to silently suffer through from the privacy of my own bed, or bathroom, or car.

Sharing a life with V and witnessing firsthand the high highs and low lows of individuals with bipolar I opened my eyes to a frightening, exhausting, exhilarating world of mental health awareness and advocacy. Mania and other extreme manifestations of mental illness are not as easily hidden as my aforementioned struggles, but society at large gawks at and passes judgment on anyone experiencing such issues rather than holding a compassionate space for them. This stigma makes it very easy to give up hope. And tragically, people give up hope all the time.

So, what alleviates stigma and restores hope? Awareness, education, compassion, connection, community, and resources. I've seen all of these at play in V's mental health journey, not because they magically appeared (though privilege is definitely a factor), but because V and her loved ones work incredibly hard on facilitating a loving and supportive environment at all times. This is possible because of V's willingness to be open about her experiences—the good, the bad, and the ugly.

V's vulnerability sends a powerful and healing ripple effect into the world that benefits everyone in her path, myself included. Her honesty made it easier for me to speak up about my own mental struggles. Her resilience inspired me to be brave in the darkest and scariest moments of my life. Her ability to build community has taught me that chosen family is essential to survival and well-being. I will never forget these lessons. I use them every day.

Spending a lot of time under her own microscope, V meticulously examines the extremes of herself, observing the slight and significant ways her mind and her world is affected by genetics, relationships, medications, you name it. Through her work, she gives us a glimpse of these findings. Only, when *we* gaze through the lens, it feels more like looking through a telescope. Vast. Unfamiliar. Beautiful. Scary. Other times, it feels like looking into a mirror. Intimate. Familiar. Beautiful. Scary. Thank you, V, for helping me see the world and myself more clearly. I know this book will do the same for so many people.

Who am I, what qualifies me, and will you like my jokes?

Hi, I'm Veronica aka "V." First of all, I'm not brave. The events you will read seem like things that took bravery but my hand was forced. I didn't have a choice and it wasn't bravery—it was bipolar I. It was my raging, gorgeous illness. My friends and my family, those are the brave ones. Bravery, to me, is staying when you don't have to. I didn't have a choice, but they did.

I'm finally writing this section of the book. Even though it is one of the first sections, it is the last thing I am writing at the tail end of the summer of 2023—now forty and feeling stable. I have had seven years of respite from major manic episodes. I've been able to stop myself from going to the hospital more times than I can count on my fingers and toes. This has been the longest break between episodes. I wonder when the next one will hit. I wonder if I'm manifesting "going crazy" on the nights it wakes me up in the way I wake from my sleep, realizing someday I'm going to die.

I wrote this book because my friends and family would hear my stories from pure unadulterated mania and say things like, "You've got to write this down." I started seeing the value in my story more and more. Slowly, I realized that sharing one person's tragedy can actually do a lot of good in this world. By sharing some of my most embarrassing, cringey, unhinged moments in living with bipolar I, maybe others with this diagnosis could feel a little less embarrassed and cringe. Maybe it will help them realize it's okay to unhinge.

To the people reading this book who are diagnosed with bipolar—it's not all our fault, loves. And it is unfortunate that our loved ones can't always be inside our minds to see what is our responsibility and what is out of our control.

I didn't realize, but in interviewing those most directly affected by my illness, I was allowing them to speak what they may not have always felt safe to speak with me. I uncovered things I did that I do not remember doing.

Live from my kitchen in Fort Collins, Colorado, I'm reflecting on the decade of work this book took me. It started as twenty-one interviews I transposed meticulously—questions I needed answered. I wanted to know if what I thought happened during the times of my hospitalizations really happened that way. Some of my experiences felt too hard to believe. I talked to my best friends, family, therapist, and psychiatrist, and sometimes I got answers I didn't want. Sometimes I got let in on truths about myself that for years remained out of the scope of my awareness.

In short, if you want the dirt on yourself, go get a recording device and ask around. You might be surprised by what you find. We all have some story to offer the world and this is mine. If you're wondering about the title of the book, go ask a Catholic why it's funny.

What to expect from this book:

This book outlines three major manic episodes. It explores those episodes from three vantage points:

1. The person with mental illness—in this book, me mostly and an interview with my buddy Alex who also has bipolar I.
2. The Caretaker—in this book, my community of friends from California like Lindsay, Christine, and Noelle, who are the most prominent in this book, and my family like my sisters Steph, Krista, my mom, and my brother from Colorado.
3. Mental Health Team—in this book, my psychologist, Dr. R, and my psychiatrist Dr. E.

I interviewed people who witnessed the breaks and compared their stories with mine leading up to, during, and after my psychotic stages, to see if the stories were the same and to be shown what it's like to be on the other side. To be the person watching the psychotic or depressive episode.

By looking back on the stories told in this book, I'm realizing there were moments I blacked out. Part of this may have been due to the higher levels of medications I had to be on during that time. Much of my recollection is valid, but there are so many holes in my memory during which other things had taken place. I also realized there was an element of distortion that happened in my perceptions during mania. Regardless of the facts in each event, what I experienced was real to me.

I requested and reviewed over seven years of therapy notes from Dr. R to watch for patterns. I wrote a snippet of this book at the height of a psychotic break. While I was in the process of writing this book, I had my third manic episode.

This book is designed to inform and inspire people with mental illness, caregivers, and mental health teams. This book is meant to smash stigma and clarify assumptions people have about what it's like to live with a mental illness. The spine of this book is built on hope.

This is my account of living with bipolar I. There are many other ways to live with it. Duration and severity of all aspects of bipolar I vary from person to person. I understand that being white and middle class have been to my advantage. In order to protect people, some information is left out. I have notated certain words with asterisks (for example, "s*icide") in case seeing those words complete is triggering. Trigger warnings for those who have contemplated s*icide and/or experienced mania and depression.

1

Genesis

W*here am I? Who are these people?*

I'm lying down. They are talking to each other. It's three or four people. I can't open my eyes completely. I can't hear. They are wearing long white jackets. They are doctors. It's dark in this room, but I can see the white. Why can't I move my arms? *I'm strapped down! They are going to do surgery on me with no anesthesia! I can't move!*

This kind of thing happens to other people. This happens to people much older than me on the streets or maybe only in the movies.

I'm dead, and I'm in a small room in hell. They are going to torture me like this for eternity. There is nothing I can do now. I am powerless.

This doesn't happen to normal people.

I can't speak. What is on my face? Something is strapped to my face! What is on my wrist? I look down at the white bracelet on my wrist. "Jane Doe, twenty-eight" is written across it.

I am not dead! I am reincarnated. My name is now Jane and I'm twenty-eight.

That early San Diego morning in the hospital, I was gifted another brain. A brain that didn't feel anything like the one I always had. Since then, I've had both brains. On rare occasions, they coexist, crammed into my skull with little room for anything but thoughts. Other times, they are independent. One is inside my head, and the other is hidden in my closet next to the trekking poles I never use.

2

Back to School

"There are many types of mental illnesses. Anxiety, schizophrenia, depression…"

Another lecture from my professor, another class required to get my bachelor's degree.

"When music therapy is applied correctly…"

Pacing back and forth in the front of the classroom, I stared at our Psychology of Music professor, who also happened to be the chair of the Music Theater and Dance department. It was like watching a slow yet aggressive tennis match. His thick German accent punctuated his points. He had spikey white hair, a sensible mullet, and almost exclusively wore black turtlenecks when the Northern Colorado cold came in with the changing of the seasons.

"The next mental illness we will be studying is bipolar disorder."

Bipolar disorder—age twenty-one was the first time I recall hearing that term. This was four years before my very own first manic episode at twenty-five—a junior in college. I was in the front row all the way to the right and there were about fifteen other Music Therapy majors sprinkled throughout the room.

I was probably wearing my infamous brown cargo shorts with as many pockets as I had pairs of Chaco sandals (many), my brown beanie to help cover the patch of hair I constantly pulled from my head, with brown eyes to match, long brown hair tossed in to a messy ponytail, and thin, poorly drawn on brown eyebrows. The sun paled with the season and my once olive complexion went back to its whiter, colder, drier phase.

My professor prompted us: "We are going to draw a simplified graph that shows what a mood cycle in bipolar I can look like. Draw a horizontal line at the bottom of the paper. Now from left to right, draw a line that goes up rapidly. Once you get to the top of the paper, draw a line rapidly descending."

As instructed, I pressed my pen down. Extreme highs and lows that are generally heavy on the high, not to mention psychotic features like delusions, which simply put, are beliefs that don't seem to be based in fact or reality. For example, in my case, in all my episodes so far, I have had the delusion that I am Jesus at the second coming and I have to end my life to save all of humankind. No pressure, V.

My teacher continued: "Another type of psychotic feature is paranoia." In my case, believing someone is recording my conversations or plotting to end my life, while in reality, I am at the grocery store and a stranger just happens to glance up at me.

"Another psychotic feature is hallucinations." In my case, more so audio hallucinations and sometimes visual hallucinations. For example, when I think someone is whispering in my ear or someone's eyes change to look like a lizard's eyes, with an eyelid that closes from left to right, when no one else is perceiving the same sights and sounds.

Sitting in class, I visualized what someone with bipolar I would be like. I figured people like that could only be contained by four padded walls and never able to contribute much. They couldn't ever find a space of balance and could never be fully trusted.

My pen lifted. My eyes studied the simplified version of this experience that others endured. "I'm glad I don't have that," I thought.

3

The South Side of Mania

I was young, too young to understand what depression was.

I was ten years old, sporting an early '90s perm and a violent banana yellow-colored sweat suit. I was in the music room of my childhood home, sitting on the ledge next to the fireplace, experiencing my first major depressive episode, and I don't know if anyone even noticed. Looking back, I think I hid it well.

I was the class clown. I was loud and ready to crack a joke at any moment (still always ready for a pun). Then that winter hit. As a kid, depression manifested in a different way. It felt more physical. My body ached, and I felt slow. Almost catatonic. The way my eyes tracked things felt slow. My speech felt slow, and I felt stupid. I was depleted and pale.

Even the daylight was muffled. Many nights on the wide-open Eastern Plains of Colorado, I would sit by the fireplace with my head hung between my legs—the drone of local news coming from the next room. The tiny farm town would have mourned for me had they only known. Nothing and no one could keep me company.

As a child, I hadn't heard of depression, so the unknowing was the scariest part. Not knowing something makes it a lot harder to find. To identify and to get help. It's like looking in a bag full of things and forgetting what you are looking for…until you remember, "Oh, right! My wallet," you will just search aimlessly.

My childhood ran in slow motion. That may be especially true in a rural community with not as many distractions that make the present moment even shorter. Byers, Colorado, population of under 1,000, graduating class of thirty-three. I remember days I would be in the wheat field with my siblings, pulling rye or laying down irrigation pipe, running across the prairie, riding my bike around the house, slowly learning to play my mom's piano, eating a homemade meal with the family every night, not thinking about the past and not worrying about the future. Living moment to moment. By bedtime, it felt like a week had passed. But in depressions, it was as if twenty years had passed. Like I had been dropped in a vat of corn syrup. I don't remember how I got out of it. For all I know, it could have only lasted a week.

About a decade passed. I don't recall ever being overwhelmed by emotion or imbalanced for extended periods of time. Nineteen years old hit and so did my second depression. I was a happy young adult who had forgotten about that gray cloud from all those years ago. I remember the exact moment it hit this time. Six kids and two parents were seated inside a minivan on the way to some airport in Wisconsin. I was in the back seat. My mom looked at me from the front seat and said, "Veronica, do you have your license?" I opened my wallet, looked at my license and that was that. It felt as if I was in a movie. As if I were on a big empty stage with no one there to care with no voice left to speak with. It felt like what nothing might feel like at first. But then, the ache. Touched again by depression. The minivan rolled down the highway and my family was probably having casual conversation, nothing seemed to change, but for me, everything changed. There was no explanation. No reason. Depression stole my life-force for the second time. Call it genetics, chemicals, crappy luck, or an extreme and bizarre case of car sickness, it was back to the shadows for me.

To me, this is the difference between depression and sadness: Sadness is something that logically happens. A dog dies—that makes you feel sad. You hurt a friend's feelings—that makes you feel sad. There are things that can trigger sadness into depression. People, especially those who have a predisposition to depression, could have their emotions turn on them for no reason. On vacation on a beautiful island, at a basketball game, on the top of a rollercoaster, or in a minivan on the way to some airport in Wisconsin.

While I was a sophomore in college, I thought about s*icide a lot. I could end my life with anything, I recall thinking. I would be walking and a bus would whiz by. I could run in front of it. I would be driving in the mountains and "I could just swerve off" would enter my mind.

No one really knew what to do. Especially me. I failed a few classes that semester and found my way to the campus therapist. My mom wrote a list on a green piece of construction paper. It's called "how to stay up." I've hung that list in the closets of eight homes over the years. Sometimes I stand in the closet and read it. To be clear, I always come out of the closet. More on that later.

The list says:

1. Don't overcommit
2. Sometimes do nothing
3. Eat healthy
4. Learn to say, "no"
5. Organize clutter
6. Make a list for daily activities
7. Stay involved
8. Get enough sleep

9. Be with friends
10. Challenge yourself
11. Realize no matter what happens things will be ok

There are spans of time in which looking at my mother's handwriting is the only thing that can keep me afloat in a lonely, helpless moment. Knowing they are loving, feeling words from a loving mother. My mom. The cloth from which I was cut. It helps remind me of how I can help myself when mom isn't around. When it doesn't matter who is around because nothing feels like enough. No human or thing feels like enough comfort or consolation. The words are there on those faded pieces of construction paper, currently hung in my kitchen cabinets where the mismatched plates, glasses, and bowls live. The cursive letters are my guide and gentle reminder to pick something that can help out of the list and try it.

There wasn't anything anyone could do to take the weight off my shoulders. Worse, people were noticing. I had a class in which I had to interview a professor. During the interview, my chemistry teacher stopped me mid-sentence and said, "Are you depressed?" I could do nothing but cry. I got help, took medications, and with time, it left.

I came into my junior year of college, and a lot changed for me. The two biggest things being my major and my awareness around my sexual orientation. I look back and laugh at both of these things. I had a deep love for music and a deep love for girls as a child. Somehow, I was a business major dating men my freshman year. Getting into Music Therapy and women my junior year just confirmed what I had always loved and known.

Dating men turned into dating women on a fateful December night with five too many shots of peppermint schnapps. The only time I would have to thank alcohol for showing me what my mind refused to admit sober. I don't remember my first kiss with Hallie, a memory I would have loved to keep. But I do remember waking up in her arms on my favorite Sunday to that date.

The newfound courage I felt gave me some of the push to follow the things I really believed in. The things that I was good at. I changed my major for the last of five times to Music Therapy with a little glimmer of hope and a lot of desperation. In order to join the major, I had to try out on my instrument of choice. I remember staring blankly at the Snare Etude, like random notes blurted onto a page. "I can do this…I've been playing percussion since elementary…" I was in my car, imagining another failure in tears that blurred the notes into a gray. "What. Am. I. Doing." I entered the room where my professor would grade my performance. A sweaty set of drumsticks that I clung tightly to with my shaking hands. I don't remember anything about what I sounded like, but I did well enough and I found myself in my first class of my actual major: Intro to Music Therapy.

I was sitting there waiting, wondering. "Well, hopefully, this class explains what Music Therapy is…"

4

Meet Alex

Alex:

"The body gets burnt out. I was in bed a lot. I don't know how to push myself out of it. Your body is in a different state. You can't force it to be in another."

Alex is a tall, thin, twenty-something, gentle giant who sometimes thinks he is Kim Jung Un, Superman, or Satan, depending on the day or delusion. He has pale pale skin and dark dark hair. As if the extremes in his mind match the contrast of his physical features. He has a serious face and a wonderful laugh.

I was in my early thirties when I met Alex. We looked like each other that night. Both wearing black-rimmed glasses, a short fade, and button-up shirt. Buddy Holly at a quick glance. Alex was in the crowd, and I was looking back from the stage. During most of my shows I mention having bipolar I, and I write songs about it. After my set, his mom introduced us—someone like me. I'd never met someone with bipolar I outside of a hospital stay and I asked him how it all felt.

"I feel demonic. Like I'm possessed by a demon. I'll go into the bathroom and roar. My eyes look mesmerizing. Sometimes, when I wake up, I feel like a demon rushed into me or rushed past me."

The feeling of possession has come over me in mania, sometimes in depression, and sometimes in a regular state. It usually happens when I am in public and there are a lot of people around. It also happens at night when I'm driving. Small, dark, busy spaces like music venues and bars can be a recipe for disaster. Alex understood this.

"I can feel people's energy on a cell level. I don't know if it's a spiritual energetic thing that is happening. Now, I don't feel like that. But manic, I feel everything in the room, in drawers, in books. I would pick up a book I was energetically drawn to. I would open the book and a line would be there that would speak to me."

Alex is eight years younger than I am, yet he has had twice the number of episodes.

"In all my episodes, it has been three months mania and three months depression.

After my manias I get depressive episodes. It's only after mania. The depressions have been getting worse. It's a different kind of depression. It's not very mental. It's bodily. I burn out. It's probably the same kind of depression someone on meth would get if they stopped using."

5

The Alley Next to Target

Eyes closed, no shoes, no keys, no wallet, sober as a judge, fresh urine (made by yours truly) in my blue sweatpants because bathrooms are for the weak.

In the darkened "wee" hours of May 4, 2008, my delusions were set loose on the streets of North Park in San Diego. It seemed to be right on time, as the onset for manic episodes in people born female is twenty-five years old.

Maestro, please cue the italics so the reader knows when it's Manic Veronica talking:

The alley. That is where I will find it. That is where I will find death in order for all to live. Here in this empty parking spot. The telephone line is about to fall on the car, which is going to explode. I know it is my time to go. This is the way it is meant to be. This is how I will find my way out. To be free and to free others.
Let go, Veronica.

With my arms outstretched, much like the way Jesus looked during his crucifixion, I fell backward, hitting my head on the parking stopper, resting there.

There is a fresh wound on the back of my head. I can feel the warmth of blood slowly traveling down my neck.

At least I thought that was what happened.

Let go. Get to the other side. You will be safe.

It seemed every second passing came with a new emotion. A new thought.

A man's voice. There is a man lying next to me. He is yelling at me.

"HEY!"

Do not respond. Do not move. Keep your eyes closed. He might come and try to physically open them.

"HEY, LADY!"

Maybe the man was a person experiencing houselessness wondering what was going on. Maybe he was the one to contact the ambulance. Maybe the man wasn't real. I had been out there in that alley all night. I just kept my eyes closed as long trains of senseless thought collided against one another like bumper cars.

I didn't move. I didn't say a word. It was all happening in my head. I imagine it from the outside now. What would someone else have seen?

I hear a heart monitor bouncing off the building wall in front of me. It's my heart. It's slowing down. Finally, I have lost all of my blood, and I'm going to die. The heart monitor goes flat. A long tone. That's it.

Tires on pavement. Engine shuts off.

"Ma'am! Ma'am can you hear me?"

Stay calm.

They rub my sternum. I don't feel anything.

Do not react.

"Ma'am!"

Keep your eyes closed.

"She's faking it."

They put me on a gurney.

This is it. I made it. All my life, I feared going to hell. The day is here, and I'm going to heaven! The people around me are angels. They are making sure I make it safe. It's going to be a long ride.

"Ma'am we are putting an IV in your arm."

Wait. These are not angels. They are demons! They are trying to poison me. This isn't the ride to heaven. It's the ride to hell!

Terrified and devastated.

I have to do something.

I ripped the IV from my arm. I remember shoving something up my nose.

"HEY!"

Someone is shoving something up my nose.

Maybe it was to stop the bleeding in the ambulance.

I can't tell what it is because I can't open my eyes. They will steal my soul if I open my eyes. I'm going to hell. I'm going to hell. I can't escape this. I must try. Keep your eyes closed.

I'm so tired. I need to get out of here. Where am I?

6

Finding the Lost

"Yes, we have a woman that fits that description."

After much detective work, three friends got a hold of a hospital that had an unidentified Jane Doe who had involuntarily checked in through the emergency room. One of those friends was Christine.

Christine was one of my first friends when I moved to San Diego about a year prior to this break. She is the mayor of most of her friend groups. A loyal, consistent, trustworthy person, and luckily one of my closest friends. Growing up in Puerto Rico, she finally made her way to San Diego, where she still lives with her wife and kiddo.

My friend group was growing and everyone was getting to know me. They didn't know this shoeless, pee-pants, confused woman who walked to the alley late at night in search of death. Nor did I know this woman screaming in the ambulance, shoving things up her nose, and spitting at people out of fear.

The long night in the alley turned into a long morning for my friends.

Christine recalls:

"I started getting texts really early the next morning. Our group of friends just stayed at their houses, hoping you would come to one of the houses. Then we all split off. I looked at a bunch of churches. I asked people if they had seen you. I went back to your house after that, which was home base for our friends."

I sometimes think about what it must have felt like to be in my friend's shoes. To not know if your buddy is alive or dead. Safe or in harm. To have no control but to call hospitals and hope.

Christine arrived at the hospital.

"The (hospital) staff asked us to come see you to identify you. When we saw you, you were tied up, your arms were tied, you had a mask on your face because you had been spitting on people, and you were out. The doctor asked if you had done drugs before, and we knew you hadn't. He then told us you had a psychotic episode.

"We were just there, touching you, talking to you, and just being with you. They probably sedated you because you were kicking and screaming and spitting. We all stayed at the hospital. The whole crew was there. They then transferred you to the behavioral health unit, and we waited until we could see you."

I don't remember any tangible struggles that would have led me to all of this madness. The biggest thing on my plate at the time was my job. My caseload as a Music Therapist was way too big but I didn't know better. It was normalized. I was fresh out of an internship and just wanted to do my best.

Before this first episode, it seemed to be the same thing day in and day out. Wake up around 6:30 a.m. after a late night of playing music somewhere, put on makeup over the top of the makeup I had on the day before, pick out a dress, put on some pumps, and get to work. Get home late, chain-smoke Parliament Lights in my living room while staring off through the wall, play music, rinse, repeat.

Christine was learning more and more about being the manager for my band and was still getting a gauge on my aspirations. Leading up to the break, my confidence was through the roof.

"From your perspective, everything was flying in your music career. Everything was going really well, and you had all these connections. Really big ideas. At this point, I had only known you for a year. The only Veronica I knew was the super funny, high energy, stay-up all night writing songs, crazy on-stage friend that I had. You would talk about how you were going to do a big concert for autism, and you were going to open for Jason Mraz," Christine said.

Then the milk spoiled.

"Weeks before the episode, you got really depressed. You were just crying and crying. Inconsolable. A deep sadness. We started going with you to look for churches. It felt like you were looking for something."

7

Nun the Wiser

I grew up in the Catholic Church my grandfather helped build in 1972 on a land he helped plow until he was no longer strong enough to do so. My mother was the church organist at the age of fifteen and over fifty years later, she still sits on that small wooden bench. Once I got old enough and brave enough, I joined the church choir. The final push was hearing my mother tell me, "God gave you gifts to use them." And if there is one gift I know I have, it's music. We had a convincing, charismatic teen life leader at the time who taught us all about Catholicism. He was charming and magnetic. It really ignited the fire in me. I was in love with it all.

I prayed the rosary at least once a day, had an altar in my bedroom, and would practice self-infliction rituals as penance during prayer. Whether it was me kneeling on my drumsticks I used during band practice, or a brush, or tightening a belt as hard as I could around my ribs. I was convinced I was a sinner and could never truly deserve the love of my Creator. In my church, penance was power. I had to do anything and everything in my power to join Him after death.

I was a good kid who constantly thought about the sins she had. For example, I remember at sixteen confessing through tears that a boy kissed me on the cheek. I felt dirty and awful about it. The priest made me say ten Hail Mary prayers as a penance. I prayed them through shameful tears.

I knew a lot about the Catholic faith. I didn't realize I was gathering so much fodder for my future manic episodes. When I'm manic, my delusions are very religious and biblically accurate. Everyone is a character from the bible or is somehow religiously associated in my mind.

At seventeen, I asked my mother if we could visit a convent. I wanted to join the sisterhood. I was about thirty years younger than any of the nuns in the cloister. When we left my mom said, "Go to college and get an education first. Then, if you still want to be a nun, you can join."

I went to college and became a lesbian instead.

8

Veronica Is Gone

Once I got to the unit, I was settling in. There were three units in the behavioral health facility and the one I was in was called the south unit. The south unit was more for people who attempted s*icide, older adults, people with dementia, and/or people with developmental delay.

Christine was one of the people that came to visit.

"First two nights, you were still Veronica. You were asking us what had happened. You kept asking if you were bleeding on the back of your head. You were so disoriented, but you were still you," Christine said.

I thought the south unit was "purgatory." In the Catholic religion, it is believed that many people go to purgatory before they can go to heaven. It's a middle ground. There is a lot of suffering in purgatory, but, in my opinion, it's better than eternal flesh-burning fire.

Christine:
"You were like the mayor of the floor. Everybody knew you. You said hi to everyone."

There were about twenty rooms on the unit floor, and the unit was one big square so it was easy to go room to room. That's just what I did. The nurse told me I had to be asked in to rooms as I had been just entering. I followed the "new" rules, knocked, and entered each room. I had memorized every person's name on the floor.

No one can wrong me. I am love, and I have a specific mission in life.

I must save these souls from this place. I have to tell them the good news of God. I have been receiving messages directly from God.

I remember making one of the patients cry. I don't remember what I told them.

She is crying for joy from this message from God.

Looking back this woman may have had dementia. I could have confused her further or even scared her.

I have saved her.

Nurse:
"Veronica, you have visitors."

Around fifteen people came to this particular visit. It all came to a head on day three during a visitation with Christine.

"I came in and said, 'Hey, Veronica.' You said, 'I'm not Veronica. Veronica is gone. I'm God.' It was funny and terrifying at the same time. You were dead serious. We needed you to sign this paper with my name on it, but you put everyone's names on it because you thought they were your disciples. You finally just had to sign your name and you signed 'God' in cursive. I left your room and went to the waiting room and just bawled. We had no idea if you were ever coming back. You were gone," Christine said.

My disciples! They are here! They cry for joy that they have seen the goodness of the Lord!

One after another I thought I was convincing my friends that I was God. A few cried. I took what they said and did and contorted it.

I was fluidly moving from one religious' figure to another, depending on the person and what I felt their personalities or behaviors most lined up with the bible. I thought I was one of three entities: God, Jesus, or The Holy Spirit. In the Catholic religion, this is known as the Holy Trinity. Three in one. Sort of like two-in-one shampoo and conditioner with the same amount of mystery in how it all works.

Disciple, angel, demon, or other holy figure—during the hospital visitation I labeled my friends accordingly.

My friend, Rachel, kissed me on the cheek when she left.

She is Judas. I cannot trust her.

Judas was one of Jesus' disciples. Judas kissed Jesus in a crowd and exclaimed, "Rabbi" to reveal Jesus' identity. The crowd arrested him and sent him off to crucifixion. Even though Judas' birth gender was male and Rachel's birth gender was female, I made sense of it merely because of the kiss. I was looking at everything through the lens of the bible and the teachings I was given growing up. Religious delusions are common in mania for a lot of people, mine just had a lot of accurate (to the bible) details.

My friends Molly and Andrea walked in.

Satan and a fallen angel.

Molly and I are close friends. She's magnetic, has short hair, and is very tall. Much like I would imagine Lucifer in my manic state. This episode was at the beginning of our friendship. I see a lot of similarities between us. In the way I see Molly's darkness, she can see mine and holds space for it in my deepest times of need. We are also the friends who would sneak a cigarette and an extra shot in our twenties, so maybe my mind made her Satan for those reasons. No one wants to be Satan in their friend's religious delusions but someone has to do it. Molly's eyes even looked demonic to me during the visit.

I deemed my friend, Andrea, as a fallen angel as she was the one with Molly—Guilty by association.

Visitors left, visitors came in.

Of all the visitors that day, there were two that were most important and crucial, not only in my delusions but also in reality.

This is John the Baptist, my closest confidant, and Mary, my wife.

I probably thought Christine was John because Jesus and John were very close, as Christine and I are. John always showed up for Jesus. Every time I've had an episode since I have thought Christine was John. John was always loyal to Jesus and would do anything to help his friend.

The important, and somewhat complex, religious role was for my stronger-than-steel, sweeter-than-honey partner at the time, Noelle.

Mary.

Noelle came into my life like a meteor. I met her in the parking lot of Humphrey's, a venue I used to play in. I felt like I was in a movie as she walked toward me, approaching the venue. She was stunning and she still is. She was a Music Therapy intern who happened to be working at the same place I interned two years prior. That night, she felt familiar and like someone I'd never met all at the same time. The only way in which she paled was her fair complexion. Her lively eyes and radiant smile were always there to tell me all is well. She had a tender and dark singing voice that drew me in. The perfect blend of Midwestern kindness and authenticity, where she grew up, and West Coast mindfulness that she seemed to embody. The night I met her I knew we would be together someday.

The hospital visitation on the third day must have been one of the first times I had seen Noelle since the night before my break.

Noelle:
"You did **not** want to see me. Other friends came to visit you at that time. I was always there, but I rarely saw you the first couple days."

After a long day for all, Noelle and Christine were called into a mandatory meeting.

Christine:
"Noelle and I needed to be there for the seventy-two-hour hold. The patient advocate team was there: psychiatrist, psychologist, social workers, and other staff. It was very official. We were meeting to see if they were going to release you. You were all smiles in the meeting. We were going around the table saying our names. When we got to you, with a smirk on your face you said, 'Veronica May.' Then they continued, and you interjected, 'Actually, I'm God.'"

Spoiler alert: They didn't release me.

I can't remember sleeping during those days in the south unit. Endlessly, I paced the halls like a metronome—back and forth. I avoided all reflective surfaces.

I know I am in Veronica's body, and if I see Veronica's body through the eyes of God, I will perish.

I went back to my room and faced a mirror made of metal. I looked down at my body but not my eyes. I slowly moved my head up to see my stomach, my chest, my neck to chin. Finally, inches from the dull metal mirror, under a fluorescent light, we locked eyes. The eyes of Veronica believing she is looking into the eyes of God. *My eyes have a burnt caramel brown center with red lightning bolts darting the circumference with a yellowish, fuzzy exterior.* I stared so hard and so long into those eyes that I fell into some other place, and I don't know what brought me back.

My face was like the bark of an old oak tree. A rough, caramel brown, unmoving. I didn't recognize this person. Staring long enough it was as though I was looking at a picture of some crazy woman in history. Observing her as if she was not me. I could see this was the beginning of something wonderfully awful. I stayed like that through twilight.

The gift of morning swept the curse of the night away.

9

Way to Go, Noelle

*W*ho *is sitting at the top of my stairs? Wait. What? Why is Noelle here? How am I going to do this if she is here?! I need to get to the knives so I can let the light out of this body I'm in!!*

Noelle may have saved my life the night before my break. I was not pleased with her because of it. I was in tunnel vision and saw the only solution as going to my home and essentially stabbing myself to possible death. Noelle being at the top of my stairs was preventing me from following through on this delusion. The knives were past her, through the door. This must have been the reason I refused to see her in the hospital. Prior to the knife moment, the night before my first hospitalization, we were at a party together and I had driven to the party alone. Looking back, I'm not sure how I drove myself in that state.

I was in more than hypomania, and I was reading into every sign on the street, every song on the radio in my car. For days on end, before my break, this was the case.

There is a roadblock up ahead. It's a sign that this party I'm going to may not be safe. I'm not supposed to go. I need to go home. Wait, a "detour" sign, which tells me I'm meant to keep going.

The line I crossed from lucid to manic seemed invisible. I didn't question my thoughts, and I don't remember the first moment they turned on me. It was like I was asleep in the middle of some nonsense nightmare, but I was fully awake.

I got to the party at Nikki's house. It was our first (and last) no-talent show. A place for us all to perform something we were not good at. I don't think there was any turning back from heading into a break.

Almost all of my friends are here, and I feel alive. I look the best I have ever looked and everyone wants to talk to me. Everyone's eyes look different, like they are dilated. They know I can see into them and they can see into me. I see beauty, and they see beauty.

Christine saw something different.

"At the party, you were super weird. I remember your eyes looked crazy and glazed over. When people would perform and people would laugh, you would get really serious. 'You guys! This is really hard for them!' When you laughed, you'd laugh too hard. Everything was too much."

As the party was winding down, I was winding up. Before leaving, I made sure to have an intimate talk with each person. *These will be my last conversations so I want them to be special and memorable.*

My thoughts and moods were not smoothly transitioning from one moment to the next. Like a light switch, the night turned on me suddenly.

Everyone is looking at me. Why is everyone staring at me? They are all talking about me. I think the night sky could come crashing down on me. I need to go home. Kitchen knives. I have kitchen knives and then this will be over.

I drove home like a zombie. I was hyper focused and coming to terms with what I believed to be my impending doom.

I didn't call it killing myself.

I need to release all the light trapped inside me. The only way to let the light out is by poking holes in my body—inside is the light of God.

What looks like one thing to an outsider may look completely different through the eyes of someone who is manic, someone who is profoundly depressed, or someone struggling within. The outsider would have found a girl deceased in her living room with a rusty knife from Target in her hand. They may have assumed I was tormented or that I was selfish for leaving friends and family with the aftermath of grief. What I saw was liberation, what I saw was necessary for the world to go on. I didn't want to end my life; just let the light out, and my thoughts stopped there.

If it's true that we hurt the ones we love the most, Noelle must have been a great love of my life. When I interviewed her later, she said:

"I don't remember what we were fighting about, but when we got back to your place, we were in your kitchen and you got really angry. You shoved me into the cupboard, and it caught you by surprise, and you kissed me. I was still mad, so I walked away, and you threw me into the fridge. I said, 'What are you doing?' This was so not you. You just ran. I assumed you were at the bottom of the stairs calming down. All your stuff was still in the house."

I do not remember getting aggressive or kissing Noelle. My recollection was different.

Noelle is getting closer to me. I need to get her out of here. She is starting to read my mind. I will go into the kitchen. She's backing me into the corner. Don't look in her eyes. She is trying to suck out your soul through your eyes. Her eyes are black now. I cover my eyes with my hands and tell her to go away. I'm scared. I run past her and out of the house.

I ran as fast and hard as I could.

What Noelle thought was going to be a few minutes of cool-off outside soon became something more. She must have known this was more than a fight.

"I felt weird. I knew something was wrong. As time passed, I knew you weren't just going to clear your head."

I was walking the night streets of North Park. I felt very confident in where I was going.

Alex:
"In mania, I have felt like I was being led by something in the sky, and it was pulling me forward."

Something is moving me left and right, forward and backward. My feet are leading me into this alley, it's the dead of night. Everything is quiet, I am safe now. It's time, Veronica. God, here I come.

10

Go to Hell, North Unit

That time I got sent to hell. It was only half bad because I met my therapist there.

Dr. R:
"When I first saw you, it was in passing. You were on the north unit. The north unit usually had a lot of people experiencing houselessness. That unit is usually for people who are more aggressive, more people who have hallucinations and a lot of delusions. It is a male-dominated unit. I remember making a note that there was a young woman on that unit. Even though you were dazed, you looked put together, so you stuck out."

Dr. R was my therapist for almost fifteen years. Just knowing she exists in the world makes me feel a bit safer.

My descent into what I thought was hell started so innocently.

When I arrived in the hospital, I walked a lot in the south unit. Next to the nurses' desk was a button that would open the unit door into the outdoor world. The staff had to stand up to push the button. One day the door buzzed—you couldn't actually see the door from the nurses' station; it was around the corner.

I'll push the button for them.

"Thank you, Veronica."

I must talk to the people here in purgatory and I must get them to heaven. I have to save them first and then I must go out to the world. It is time to save the world, but I must start here first.

Visitation hours came and went, and the now-familiar buzz of the button sent me into help mode.

I'll push the button.

"Thank you, Veronica."

They call me by the name Veronica, but I am Jesus.

And then an idea suddenly formed.

The door is open. This is my chance. The hour is upon us. I must go to the Garden of Gethsemane. It is the hour before my crucifixion. It is time to save the world.

In the bible, the Garden of Gethsemane is where Jesus suffered greatly right before he was executed by way of being hung on a cross.

I walked out of the south unit like I owned it.

Through the doors, I'm outside. The elevator is to my left. Get in, you are almost there. I hear footsteps.

"STOP HER!"

I can make it. I am almost there. The elevator door opens, I get in, it closes and I push "1." I feel the elevator descend.

*Cue elevator music

The doors open. I get out and start walking down the hallway.

"STOP!"

It's Pontius Pilate's guards (the judge who ordered Jesus to be crucified). *They grab me by the arms, one on each side, and I surrender. My body goes limp, and I am a lamb being led to slaughter.*

While all the commotion was happening, my friends were watching through the large window in the waiting area. They saw me getting dragged off to the north unit.

Being sent to the north unit confirmed in my manic mind that I was in fact Jesus, going into the pit of hell.

I am not stopping at the living, and those stuck in purgatory. I am going to liberate the entire population that ever existed. Moments before the rapture, this is my darkest hour. This is the night I shall be crucified.

Historically, the bible says Jesus only needed to be crucified once. Then he would return "like a thief in the night" for the rapture—taking the souls that were worthy and basically releasing Satan's hounds on the others. Not actual hounds. Think fire, demons, and other things that would not be ideal. My mind was transcending time and logic. It seemed like this is how it would be from now on.

The echo of my teen life leader's words and teachings were reactivated. I was dropped into the four gospels of the bible—some of the books of the bible detailing Jesus' death.

I am weak. The guards are dragging me down the elevator. I'm almost there. I am God, I am the Holy Spirit, I am Jesus, I am the Trinity. I am not scared. I hear people screaming in the halls. It is the pit of night. Everyone is suffering. I must open the gates to heaven.

There I sat alone on my new bed, looking at the new wall. It was dark outside at this point.

Someone is coming into my room, the lights are dim. I look up from my bed, and she stares back at me. Her eyes are blue and she has red hair. It's Mary Magdalene, and she is here to seduce me.

In the bible, Mary Magdalene was said to have had red hair. There is speculation that Mary and Jesus were a thing. Talk about the pressure Mary Magdalene felt meeting **his** dad for the first time.

"Mary" was my roommate for my stay in the north unit. During my stay I slowly began to realize she was one of the most diabolical on the unit. She would shoot down the halls like a cannonball. I remember arriving at the unit and overhearing someone say, "You are putting Veronica in with **her**?"

It was very late at night, or early, depending on your perspective. I didn't have the energy or mind to care that my roommate wouldn't stop staring at me from the corner of the room. I'm sure she was in her own set of delusions.

I call for the nurse and I ask for several towels. She hands me the towels. I call the nurse "Veronica" (which, consequently, was her name).

In the bible, Veronica was one of the people standing on the road while Jesus carried his cross to the crucifixion. She walked out of the crowd toward him and wiped his face. When she pulled the cloth away, his face was imprinted on it. This cloth, known as the Shroud of Turin, is to this day in a cathedral in Italy.

So, there I was, my first night in the north unit. Up to that point, it was the scariest night of my life.

A scary night for me, indeed. Yet, I'm sure if the nurse were to have come in my room, she would have had a good laugh. There I was, head to toe covered in tiny towels, lying still on my back. If you've ever tried to delicately place little towels all over your body, then you know it isn't easy. In my mind, this was much like the way they wrapped Jesus in the tomb.

Even though I was lying there thinking I was in the tomb, after my death, I also thought I was hearing Pontius Pilate's guards from the hallways waiting to crucify me. It may have just been the screams from the other patients on the unit.

Alex B:
"I think I hear things sometimes that are not actually happening—it's screaming. When I was in the hospital, it felt like it was tied to my brain. When I started thinking about something else, the screaming would stop."

The chaos in my brain felt like a massive, thick, slow-turning tornado, picking up everything in its path.

All night I lay like this. I didn't sleep. Even though my face was covered with a hospital washcloth, my eyes were jacked open. I thought I was waiting in the jail for guards to come get me. To do the things I heard they did to Jesus in the bible: To whip me as I am tied to a pillar, place a crown of thorns on my head, and make me walk while carrying my cross to my own crucifixion. Time kept rewinding and starting over and over.

I started dissociating—feeling disconnected from who I was. I could see my body, but I didn't feel like I was in it; like an avatar. I was in a space in which I believed I was God, while being aware that the shell I inhabited was that of a twenty-five-year-old woman who went by the name, "Veronica." And I would refer to Veronica as if she was not me.

I need to get out of her body soon.

Fuzz surrounds Veronica. Her eyes won't stay focused. She's weak. There are limbs hanging in front of my sight. When she moves forward, they sway like logs hanging from twine. There are fingers hanging from the limbs. These are part of her body. Veronica's body is fading. I'll die if I don't get out soon. If I die, the whole world will pay the price. All will suffer.

Solution?

Death by body wash.

Committing s*icide in the ICU of a behavioral health unit is about as easy as baking ice cubes. We weren't allowed to have shoelaces, belts, razors, or pencils. There were no glass mirrors, just metal rectangles in which we could see our faces, but I (thought) I figured it out.

I'm going to take a shower. I will ask the nurse for two bottles of body wash.

"Do not use the stall on the right, Veronica."

We go into the bathroom and Veronica opens the curtain in the stall on the right. Blood is stained in the cracks of the grout of the tile. Someone ended their life here, it IS possible.

My eyes zoom around the room until we are in the other shower. I watch her arm lift as her hand turns the knob. It's so warm and for a moment Veronica and I become one. Her head hangs heavy, water pouring down off of the lips, nose, and fingertips.

I remember standing there like that for a long time. Like a sad, old willow tree in the center of a puddle.

I grabbed the first bottle of body wash and examined its contents. It was a bottle of white body wash. The bottle was see-through, and the cap was silver. There were probably about four to five ounces of body wash in each bottle.

I unscrewed the lid and placed it under my nose. It smelled like Motel 6 body wash.

It is toxic, but this is the only way it can be done here.

Bottles up, I squeeze the contents out into my mouth.

I feel the body wash foaming from the inside. Her throat stings as she swallows it. Her eyes are burning. I take the second bottle and do the same. I look down at her arms, her veins bulge, and skin starts slipping off. The skin is falling from her face, and I can see the veins turning a violent green. The muscles, the bones. The toxins are coursing and her heartbeats are heavy and slow.

That's it, her skin is gone. The organs and muscles are gone. All that is left is her skeleton. Her fingers slide the curtain open and her clunky bones move together to leave the bathroom. She's walking down the hall and people are looking at her. Everyone is staring in the sockets where her eyes were. The nurse runs down the hall.

"Veronica! Put a towel on!!!"

I sink back into my body.

She puts a towel around me. I don't feel good. I tell the nurse that I might throw up.

"I drank the body wash."

She looks and sounds very annoyed.

"Are you lying?"

"No."

"Here, drink this."

She hands me something in a small cup. It is white and chalky tasting. As soon as it goes down it all comes up in the kitchen trash can. As I'm throwing up, it feels like suds are coming from my mouth. I feel like I can't breathe. The nurse is towering over me.

"You know it's nontoxic, right?"

Some delusional thinking can lead to harmless nontoxic ingestions and others can be slightly riskier.

Since being diagnosed, my biggest fear is that I die a preventable death. A death caused by my mania.

There hasn't been a time in mania that I've wanted to commit s*icide. I'm always very sad that I have to leave.

11

Relax, It's Only Toilet Water

In the north unit, morning rose like a rocket, and night fell like a lead balloon. Medications, food or refusal of food, visitations, meetings, tests, and I was lost.

Noelle was going to work, coordinating visits, being a partner, somehow taking care of herself or not, while meeting with people at the hospital, and dealing with my ever-changing demeanor.

"We were in what looked like a board meeting room. They gave you a fifty-question inventory test. It was a big stack of papers, and in my opinion, the evaluation had too many questions for someone who was struggling mentally. I would have been exhausted answering it. It was to test your mental stability. You started doing the first two, and then crossed them out. Then you started making a pattern in the circles. When you held up the test answers, it was clearly a pattern. I was watching you, and I said, 'I don't think that is what this is for.' You said, 'I don't care.' You were being rebellious; whereas before, you were so low," Noelle said.

Running high or sinking low, the delusions didn't settle. I had decided the water cooler in the lunchroom was holy water.

This is the holiest water that will save everyone and reveal all truth. I had a cup I carried with me everywhere. I called it the Cup of Truth. I would drink a lot of water from the water cooler using that cup alone. I thought that the more water I drank, the more truth would be revealed to me.

These sinners must be purified. I must baptize these people with the Holy Water made ready by the Cup of Truth. I fill from the baptismal font and am ready to finally break free of the shackles upon my people's wrists and ankles. I baptize you in the name of the Father, the Son, and the Holy Spi...

"Veronica!"

What really happened...

I was calmly walking down the hall with my Styrofoam cup filled with cold-ass cooler water. I would take small sips and pace, and I'm sure I had a contemplative look on my face.

What's that? A sinner at the end of the hall.

I slowly walked toward them and took a small sip from my cup. As we passed one another, I looked over and, without warning, released the water from the cup onto faces, backs, and arms. Whatever I believed the Holy Spirit willed. When they would react adversely, I thought it was because the Holy Spirit was trying to do its work.

At least I stayed hydrated.

The screen goes black again. I wake up on the floor of my room. There is water everywhere, and I'm sopping it up with a towel—I look over.

Mary Magdalene is sopping up the water too. She must have made a mess, so I will help her clean it up.

I felt like I was in tunnel vision. Rag in my hand, water on the floor. That was all that existed in the moment.

Later on, I found out I was baptizing my room with our toilet water using that same cup I was drinking from. The staff ordered us to clean it up.

Don't all throw up at once.

12

Keep It on the Down Lo Mein

Still no sleep, and the delusions were gaining momentum. Paranoia, another form of psychosis, started manifesting in more complex ways.

They are trying to poison me. They are trying to kill me. I have to get out of here. No one will listen to me. "Please! Let us out! The water is coming! A tsunami is coming! Do you hear the water?! It's rushing toward us. Please! You have to believe me! We are going to drown!"

While I'm warning the world of its impending doom, the cook is heating up a Chinese-inspired cuisine. We all piled into the small room where we ate, did therapy, and watched TV. It was dinnertime.

We are all being poisoned with the food. I will not eat. I do not need to eat. I am the way, the truth, and the life. For the bible says, "Man does not live on bread alone." I will survive on the truth.

I didn't eat for three to five days. During the course of my fifteen-day stay, I lost thirty-five pounds.

The guards are on watch. They are going to make sure we all eat. We will all die and go to hell if we eat this food.

I looked around in every direction.

I will hide my food, so they think I've been eating.

I opened up the top of my sock.

This Chicken Lo Mein is poisoned. I'll stuff it down my socks.

The portions were decent in this hospital…

I have to stuff the rest in my underwear! It's working!

Would have been easier with egg rolls, but I'm glad it wasn't soup.

Finally. It's all hidden.

I slowly and carefully walked back to my room. I don't know how the staff didn't fall apart laughing at me but seeing odd behaviors all day must make them seem a bit more normal. I felt the squish of food in my feet and between my toes. First time for everything?

Looking back, I'm lucky I didn't get a UCI (Urinary Chicken Infection).

The best part is the staff clearly saw me doing it. I also found out patients have a right to refrain from eating. I'm sure I was a dinner topic at someone's house who worked at the hospital that night.

13

Laughter Is Medicine

I know if people look into my eyes, the eyes of God, they will perish. So too with my voice. I must spread the good news in a safe way in which people can understand and be saved. From now on, I will chant instead of speak. I must use full volume and fill the space with my almighty voice.

Noelle got a very nice performance.

"We were asking the staff if there was any way we could bring in your guitar, so you could play. You tried to sing, and it was so loud. Eight million decibels, and we are all in this tiny room. You were singing 'Hallelujah' but loud. It wasn't like a church sound. It was a funky hallelujah," Noelle said.

Another evening visitation over, and just when my vocal cords were finally warm. I saved the encore for staff members. It was an exclusive.

I remember this moment so well. I was walking down the hall singing the words "I Am Who Am" over and over.

I feel the sound resonating in my ribs with my voice, the voice of God, loud, and clear. I hear footsteps. People are running toward me from behind. "STOP." Right as I'm about to turn around, I am tackled to the ground. At least two men. My face is on the hard floor. I don't know what I have done. They carry me, chest facing the floor, limbs bent back by the arms and legs. I surrender, and I do not fight. They throw me onto my bed and one of them pulls my pants down. A syringe goes in my left butt cheek.

I let out a chant that gave the staff the go-ahead to inject the right butt cheek as well—it was my final number of the evening.

"Tuuuuuuurn the othheeeer cheeeeek."

The clouds lifted for a sweet moment; I was me. I realized how funny the statement was. The staff even started laughing out loud. I let out a hearty guffaw, and the delusions came back down on me like a pack of starved wolves. They had given me muscle injections of Abilify. I was also on lithium.

When I woke up after the injection, there was a little bit of sanity that came along with it. I went back, forth, and sometimes both at the same time. I would talk about Veronica as if she was someone else, and in the same breath, I would be Veronica. One thing was clear; the medications were slowly pushing me toward sanity. A little less paranoia, fewer delusions, and more awareness of my surroundings. The pure act of time passing helped me, but I believe it was the community of support I had around me that healed me the best.

14

Dr. Seek and Mr. Hide

I had consistent visitors and wanted to see Christine a lot. Being in crisis, I was out of the loop with the hard things she might be going through.

"After the night they injected you with Abilify, you were back to Veronica by the next day. During the visitation on the day you came back, I asked, 'Where have you been?' You walked out and started pacing the hallway. I had a lot going on in my own life at the time. This was when my cousin, Danny, was diagnosed with cancer. I had this thing going on where you had a healthy body, but your mind was gone, and Danny's body was diseased and deteriorating, but he was still there."

Noelle was working full time in a helping profession, coordinating visitation schedules with everyone messaging her about me, showing up to the hospital for me, and somehow still feeding herself.

"We went out to the smoker's lounge area. We were talking about normal stuff. At one point I said, 'Veronica, you're not God,'" Noelle said.

I so badly wanted to believe Noelle and in that moment part of me did.

"You looked at me and your whole face changed. You stood up and said, 'I'll be right back.'"

I took a walk down the hallway. I remember the thought feeling lucid. "Can I trust her?"

I turned the corner of the hallway, and my mind turned with it.

There is a man coming toward me down the hallway. A patient. It's my dad hiding in his body, coming to get me out of here.

Noelle waited in the other room as Lucid Veronica and Manic Veronica were shouting in each of my ears at the same time.

I morphed into what seemed to be one of many personas as I swaggered back into the waiting area.

"When you came back, you had a different personality. You were even walking differently; A really cocky Veronica. I said, 'Who is this?' You then snapped back and said, 'I'm sorry I don't know what happened.' You were more masculine: cocky and in control. Before you were so exhausted, tired, and scared. Now you were bright-eyed, and strutting."

What was going on in my brain?

15

Sisters

I had been in the north unit for about a week and a half when the side effects of each medication were in full swing. I had fallen flat like club soda left open for 100 years. No facial expressions, uninterested, and at moments, seemingly catatonic. Two of my sisters, Stephanie and Krista, flew out from Colorado to visit. Much of these visits were of me slumped over in a chair, mouth open and drooling, half asleep.

Stephanie and Krista are my big sisters. We skinned knees together and worked in wheat fields together. They knew funny Veronica. They knew the Veronica that walked around the house with sweat pants up to her neck saying, "I'm all legs!" Creative, coherent, "That's just Veronica," Veronica. I wouldn't have wanted them to see me this way. Reflecting, it makes me sad to think they were probably scared and sad for me.

I had requested my guitar be brought in, which was not something staff would offer in the unit. Because I was getting better, and I had such support, they snuck the guitar in and put me in a room with my sisters where we could visit in peace. They were not going to let my sister Stephanie come on to the unit as she was seven months pregnant, and that was seen as dangerous for her. People on this unit were most likely to be in psychosis and therefore unpredictable in action. With a coat in front of her, they walked in.

I was sitting on a chair and slowly looked up to see them. They were blurry at first. I had no expression. Since the medications had started working, I felt little to nothing. Not even the sight of my sisters could change my affect or make my heart feel full the way it usually would.

Krista:
"You were very withdrawn. It seemed you were masking other feelings. They let us go into a little room with you. We gave you your guitar, and you didn't want to play it the way you usually do."

My father's guitar. I wish I had asked him about more of the history of this guitar before he passed away. It was handed down to me. If you Googled "acoustic guitar" this guitar is probably the type of image that would come up. It had no physical bells or whistles. It was a medium brown Yamaha guitar, and the first guitar I'd ever played. Dad gave it to me when I was seventeen on our last official custody visit to Queens. I walked onto the airplane to fly back to Colorado to be with Mom with a guitar case clutched in my hand. I rarely loosen my grip on that guitar, as I practiced six hours a day in the beginning. I was enamored by this instrument and so curious as to what it could do. The first song I learned was "Greensleeves." I learned it by ear, as YouTube videos weren't a thing yet. The link that connected me to my father was also the link that connected me to my mother: Music. The only difference was the type of instrument they offered me and taught me along the way. I superglued an elephant to the guitar because someone once told me an elephant never forgets. I never wanted to forget my love for music. More than that, I have always been somewhat forgetful. So forgetful, that one day I forgot to take this guitar out of my car, so someone decided to take it out for me.

If you're ever at a pawnshop and see a guitar with an elephant on it, call me.

Usually when I pick up a guitar, some new melody or riff will pop out of my fingers. This day in the hospital was a bit different. The mix of meds and mania made this instrument unfamiliar.

"I don't know what to do with this right now," I thought.

I took one strum of one chord. I remember how full that guitar sounded. The strings were new, so it was shining at its brightest. I even remember the chord I played (E minor for some of you music types). My fingers felt weak, and I remember that guitar being somewhat hard to play, but in the long run, it made me a better player. One strum and feelings finally appeared and a stream of tears washed my face off. The support of others was what got me out of the hospital early but the guitar is what opened my heart back up.

I looked back through the years at dark nights when I would hit the body of that guitar out of anger or frustration, scream-singing in order to maintain balance later. Tossing it carelessly on a nearby couch or bed. I remembered the sunny days when I would lean my head on the curve of that guitar and gently awaken each string, thanking it silently for allowing me space. It felt good to cry. My sisters were having their own experiences.

Krista:
"It was very scary. I felt helpless seeing you there and not understanding. I had this feeling you'd be fine when I got there. I thought, 'Why are you in here with all these people who have problems?' It wasn't you. To see you not be who we had always known you to be was very frightening. This wasn't right. It seemed like it wasn't real. You didn't just snap out of it."

I was extremely paranoid. My delusions led me to believe I couldn't trust or talk to a lot of people over the phone.

Krista:
"You only had a couple people you would accept phone calls from. At first, I was upset that I wasn't one of the people you called. I had taken it personally up to that point. I tried to make sense of it and I couldn't."

Stephanie:
"I will never forget going to visit you in the psych unit. There was a big door with a little glass window and you were looking through the window into the hallway where I was. You had a very blank look on your face; you were pale and thin, and so not you. We visited for the time allowed and then I left, and when I left, I remember seeing your face again through that damn window and feeling so helpless because there was nothing I could do. You looked like you needed help.

"I felt so bad for you, and I was scared for you, and I just wanted to hold you, but I had to leave. Every night I was in San Diego, I slept on your couch and listened to songs you sang and recorded that were on your computer. I held your laptop and pretended it was you. I really missed you. It was nice knowing you were just a couple of miles away, but it felt like we were worlds apart."

16

Shocking: It Still happens?

I wasn't the only person on the unit that had lost her fizz.

My roommate, aka Mary Magdalene, was displaying a ton of symptoms resembling bipolar I, but I can't be sure. Fast speech, exaggerated movements, loud, delusional thoughts, and odd behaviors to name a few. During my stay several articles of clothing had gone missing. I later found out she was putting them in the toilet. It wasn't personal, and because of my new experiences, I knew it. She was experiencing a delusion. She kept thinking she had a baby in the toilet, so maybe she was trying to keep it warm.

One morning, I woke up to her straddling me. When I opened my eyes, she poured her cold cup of morning coffee on me.

The best part of waking up is Folgers on your face.

In an attempt to help and possibly tame her, they took her down the hall to get electroconvulsive therapy (ECT), which I thought only happened in the early 1900s. Apparently, ECT is used as a last resort and is very effective in extreme mania and extreme depression, especially depression (Mondimore, 2022).

I now know ECT is pretty sensationalized, as I found in my research (Mondimore, 2022), but from my personal experience and what I saw of her, before she went in, she was so animated. Before ECT, she would stomp down the halls, and seemed to have a new boyfriend every day. She was filled with a wild spirit. I actually came to like her on occasion, but she could erupt at any moment. When she came back, she was different.

    She sat down slowly on her bed. Her gaze, as if only by gravity, was on the floor, head slightly hung, fingers limply interlocked. All of her movements were slow and her face appeared extracted of all color and smoothness. Her mouth was slightly opened and her eyes were fixated on the wall. "This is what nothingness looks like in human form," I thought to myself. I had learned through overhearing staff conversations that she had been in and out of the institute many times. Sometimes I wish I could find her and meet up. Who knows? She could be back in the hospital or worse. I like to think she was able to face her demons and move on to better things.

17

Nice…Flower?

The medications slowly filled the parts of my brain that were empty and drained the parts that were overflowing.

Visitations were twice a day for about an hour each visitation. Two people could come in at a time. For the fifteen days I was there, I had at least two visitors at each visitation.

Christine:
"What struck me the most is that we would fill up the entire waiting room, and no one else would be in it. Maybe one person would be there. People were asking to come see you and we had to start making a list. You had so much support. A support system is the most valuable asset in getting out. Throughout your journey with bipolar I, you have learned that you couldn't do it alone, and you couldn't do it without the meds."

The journey in the hospital felt so long, but in reality, this was only about day nine or ten in the hospital. I was coming out of my room more often. I remember sitting in art therapy, and we were all supposed to color in a picture of flowers in a flowerpot. We all hung them up at the end of class. I looked at all the pictures and mine was the only one with "healthy" colors. My flower stem was green; my petals were orange and red. No one else had colored something that made "sense." Stems were red, flower petals were black. The art therapist came up to me and told me that it looked like I was doing better, and this was the first moment I felt like that was true. I was coming back to what would now be my new normal.

18

Tables Turned

One day, I got a knock on my door, and I was still in my hospital gown and very drowsy. I was still mildly delusional but mainly in reality. It was a man with short blonde hair and glasses who was sharply dressed in a long button-up shirt, slacks, and a lanyard that read the name, "Kyle." Kyle was the Music Therapist.

"It's time for Music Therapy."

I looked up at him and my face changed; it was one of my colleagues.

"Veronica?"

I won't forget that look of confusion on his face. As if he were wondering if **he** was the one who needed to be checked in.

"Hey, Kyle."

"What happened?"

"I'm not quite sure."

Group was about to start and that's the last time I remember seeing Kyle. Having the roles switched on me like that happened so fast. I knew what it felt like to be the client for once. I felt out of control.

I skipped out on music therapy groups and waited for cognitive group therapy. I was the only person in the group that was responding to the therapist's questions. Looking around the room, I saw one man staring in terror at the TV. I knew what was happening to him. A memory, one of many, was when we were all watching TV, and I was glued to it. Hanging on every last word, every gesture. I looked down from the TV and looked at everyone else glued to the TV. All of us looked terrified, including me. My thought was that everyone on the TV was talking to me, and I think others felt the same.

I don't remember much about what the therapist talked about in therapy that day. I do remember other people were talking to themselves, pacing, sleeping, and zoning out. I felt like some of the fog was lifting because I was starting to notice the people around me more and more. The therapist approached me afterward and said, "You look like you're doing much better. How are you handling the diagnosis?"

"What diagnosis?" I asked.

"You were diagnosed with bipolar I."

I remember feeling offended and said, "Why didn't you tell me?"

With a look of knowing and concern, he said, "Veronica, I've told you several times."

It felt like a blow to my chest. I thought I was in a dream or watching someone else's life in that moment. It hit me like it still does sometimes.

19

Dentist Chair Bed, Please

The more activities I attended, the longer I stayed out of bed; the more I showered, the more lucid I became. The more lucid I became, the more paralyzing my fear; my fear of the other patients.

There was a man in the unit that was built like a truck—muscles for miles. He had so many tattoos on his face that I couldn't really make out his facial features. I only remember two yellow hammers that stuck out because of the color, right above his eyebrows. He had what appeared to be psychomotor agitation, which is basically purposeless movements. He would shout, jump, freeze, run. Now that I was more aware and lucid, I wondered if he'd always been like this in the unit or if it was me that had changed.

Christine:
"In the north unit, I was scared. Everyone was walking around like zombies."
The vibe of the unit was not solely informed by the patients.

Krista (sister):
"The staff felt like prison guards. I was scared to leave you with them."

One night in particular, it all came to a head. I lay awake the whole night with my eyes wide open in the dark room. I heard people screaming in the hallways, people banging on doors. I imagined my roommate in the corner, just watching me, waiting to react to her thoughts.

I went to the nurse's office and begged them to let me stay in a room by myself. The only room they had was the lockdown room.

The lockdown room only had a bed with straps on it for those of us who may have gotten too physical. Once it was closed, you couldn't get out. I vividly remember the north unit doors slamming open late one night, and a man being strapped down in that room. It looked like he had been in an accident. His face was bruised and bloody. They left the door open, and I was standing outside singing, "Go to the light! Go to the light!" over and over. *The guards are trying to steal his soul before he gets to heaven!* I remember being so concerned for him. His eyes were half open and watery, as if he had been sedated—they were like two small pieces of coal with white lights in the middle. He looked confused, exhausted, and terrified. I can't imagine what that experience must have been like for him.

Alex:
"The staff were not pleasant. They would yell at you to go to your room. 'Get in the isolation room! Go, go!' One time, there was a guy chasing me with a needle to put me down. I was so paranoid I thought he would sexually assault me. They chased me around the floor and a guy got too close. I started punching him. The whole staff came and strapped me to a board and put the needle in my butt."

So, there I was, twenty-five years old, locked inside an eight-by-eight room with bare walls painted white, on a bed that was more like a dentist's chair. Just me, the chair, a pillow, and a sheet. The glow of the fluorescent lights in the hall through the tiny square window in the door kept watch over me.

Every morning I would open my eyes, hoping it was all a nightmare. My gratitude came from knowing that my fears were now (mostly) in touch with reality. I was still having moderate delusions. I think the best part was I knew where I was. I was no longer so disoriented. Now real concerns started creeping in. What was life going to look like? Was this a one-time fluke? How can I explain this to the people in my life who didn't see it happen before their eyes? How many emails am I going to have to respond to?

20

Do Better

Looking back on the intensive care unit (ICU) visits I have had, I realized that being in the ICU takes an extreme amount of mental stamina. When I put myself back in Manic Veronica's shoes, I think creating a better external environment like carpets, couches, or constant access to calming instrumental music on this unit might have decreased my stress and possibly decreased the amount of time in the hospital.

21

Going to Heaven: The Open Unit

Finally, the day I had been waiting for came: a bed was available in the open unit. This was a unit for those in least need of support. This meant a lot of different things. To name a few, it meant progress, and it meant not having to be on guard mentally and physically as much because of the state of other patients around me. The people here knew who they were and they knew where they were. Generally, there are at least two units but this hospital had three. That may be part of the reason I ultimately viewed these three places as the three places a Catholic believes they could go after they die: hell, purgatory, or heaven. In this episode, I went from the middle care to the most needed care and then to the least needed care.

The minute I set foot on the open unit, my whole body relaxed. For me, the best part of the unit was the outdoor time.

The north unit had an area with thick black screens so you could squint your eyes and look outside. Kind of like the walls put up around trampolines to keep people from flying off. I would watch the people from the south unit and open unit wander outside, walk around, play catch. I wanted to have the sun on me.

I was probably in the north unit for a total of eight days, with no sun and my body knew it. Now, I think of all the people who have been in the lockdown units like the north unit for months, for years.

I eagerly waited by the door. It felt like Christmas morning—a really shitty Christmas morning. I stood there in a line of strangers who were also grappling with their own mental health.

The staff swung the door open, and I walked down the stairs. I was overwhelmed with the outside world. There was a plot of grass that was about fifteen feet by eight feet and tall buildings that felt more like guards surrounded the outdoor space, but the sky was there. I walked to the middle of the patch of grass, and I laid down on my back with my arm behind my head. To say I felt dead inside would imply that I was feeling, but for lack of a better phrase, the dead feeling inside me was accompanied by a feeling of gratitude, perspective, and a touch of psychosis. It can be all the things at once.

My recollections of this time were a bit different from my friends and partner.

Noelle:
"You were starting to realize or see something was going on. You were seeing it, but not believing it completely. You were going back and forth between delusional Veronica and real-life Veronica. Sometimes, you were really tired and lethargic, and other times you were really excited and couldn't wait to help people on the unit."

My new roommate was a sweet sixty-ish-year-old woman whose name fails to come to me. The only way I can describe her is as a young grandma from the Midwest. She had short salt and pepper hair, comfy sneakers, and a stiff body. She had come in from a severe bout of anxiety. While she didn't know why it came on, it was unmanageable. She had never had anxiety in her life. It was to the point that she could no longer work. She moved carefully. The slightest sound or movement would scare her like a feral cat. She would startle and then freeze for minutes at a time.

Having her as a roommate gave me a feeling of purpose. I've always loved the feeling of helping someone. Maybe because I've needed to ask for help so much. It feels good to even the scale and give back when possible. I remember I would have to walk slowly, arm in arm with her to the lunchroom. I would try to initiate small talk with her to keep her mind occupied. She hated being outside of our room, and she was quite literally paralyzed by fear at times. She would stop frequently and tell me she wanted to go back, but she always made it.

One day in the lunchroom, I saw "Mary," my old roommate from the north unit. She looked tired, but she looked grounded in reality.

I said, "Hey, it's good to see you. You look better."

To which she said, "Who are you?"

I didn't take it personally because I was going through the same thing. Several staff members had approached me, calling me by name and telling me I had been doing so much better, and I probably only recognized 25 percent of them.

Around day twelve of my stay in the hospital, I started getting really antsy. From my barred window, I could see the freeway entrance. I would wait by the window sometimes, looking for Noelle's car to pass by. She made me a CD and brought me a portable CD player. I would listen to it on repeat throughout the day. I kept to myself as much as I could, and was eating and taking medications regularly. I had no idea how slow the recovery from this episode would be.

I was Veronica again. A different Veronica than I once was. I couldn't go back to old me knowing what I knew now and seeing what I had seen. I attended as many therapies as I could in the open unit. There was a therapist on the unit that really helped me lay some foundation for healing. Dr. R, who is better known as one of the best things that came out of this mess. Little did I know that she would become my long-term therapist. The one I ended up having for almost fifteen years.

Dr. R:
"When you were in the open unit is when I really knew you. That was where my rotation was. You were really into the sessions and you seemed to get it. When you do groups in the hospital setting, a lot of times, no one is listening or they can't apply things."

22

I Shall Be Released

My body was tired, but my spirits were intact. I was in a group, and the therapist was talking, while I had my eye excitedly on the clock, watching the seconds go by. I kept looking out the window, waiting to see Noelle come. It wasn't visitation time, it was release day. Every time a person walked past the registration window, my heart would jump, and I could have sworn it was her. Once I really saw her, a rush of emotions ran through me. Feelings of gratitude, feelings of triumph, and a strong sense that hope had prevailed.

Yet my excitement was hidden from my face and body. The medication seemed to cover me up.

Noelle:
"I remember you seemed really tired. You were skinny. You seemed worn out from everything. You didn't seem scared, but you seemed tentative and hesitant about what would be happening."

We slowly walked out of each set of doors and my body and mind felt slow. I moved slowly yet I couldn't wait to get outside. Outside of the four big walls that contained all the hallways, all the rooms, all the sounds, all the pain, all the confusion, and all the energy of life within it. I emerged from the final doors as a swimmer emerges from a deep dive.

When we got in the car, a Starbucks java chip smoothie was waiting for me. I remember what it tasted like. I have a sweet tooth and it almost felt like too much. It felt like such a luxury in that moment, whereas before getting a drink would just be part of my mundane day. Everything in the ICU was low stimulus, blander, dull, numbed. We drove home and got out of the car when a bus passed us, and I jumped back. Things going fast and being loud startled me. I stayed close to my house as much as I could.

Since that first day out in the "real" world, I started perceiving the world through different eyes. Eyes that felt a bit more critical, skeptical at times. Eyes analyzing their surroundings and thoughts that speak: "Am I making sense right now?" "Do people perceive me as crazy?" Assessing how safe a situation feels. Wondering how real a situation I'm a part of is with eyes on the clock thinking, "When will it happen again?"

When we left the hospital, I didn't realize that all the logistics for check-out and aftercare were just taken care of by others for me. I think of those people who leave the hospital and have to get a paid ride home or worse—no home. I don't remember checking out of the hospital or setting up my next six months of outpatient therapy. Noelle and Christine were my main care providers at this time but most of my friends pitched in one way or another.

My sister, Steph, sent me a ring after I got out of the hospital. It was silver with one word engraved on the outside of it—"Hope." I put that ring on and there it remained. I would look at it frequently when I'd get that panic feeling. "There is hope. There is hope." I would say out loud to myself.

Noelle:
"You were worried about your job and overwhelmed. You were relieved to be out, but you seemed down, and you cried a lot the first few days you were home."

I didn't even want to look at my notifications on my phone or emails. I knew that over two weeks of work and questions and texts and calls would be waiting for me. But I wasn't allowed access to any of my technology while in the hospital. I had nearly forgotten that life was still happening outside of myself.

Regardless, on the day I was released, I also remember how free I felt. My friends, Jeff and Christine, accompanied Noelle and I down the city streets of North Park. There was a lonely grocery cart on the sidewalk in front of us. I got in it, and they pushed me down the sidewalk and we laughed. Looking back at that moment, I think about the symbolic nature of it. I was allowing my friends to support me, to push me along. I finally learned to surrender and, from this experience, found ease in asking for help when it came to my mental health needs.

Life is weird sometimes. It would be a whole lot weirder without my friends and without my family.

When I got to my home, it was spotless. Sweet touches were all around to make me feel more at ease. Little notes of love, gentle reminders. I remember going to my bathroom and getting my first good look in a glass mirror since before my break, and I remember my mouth hanging open.

At twelve, I had started pulling all my eyelashes and eyebrows out, and I still do it. It's called trichotillomania, as if I needed more manias. That day in the mirror, I saw eyebrows and eyelashes. I didn't even realize they would grow back so fast. Accompanied with the hair was a slim face, emaciated. My skin looked like it was made of leather or plastic. I had difficulty with facial affect—it felt hard to smile. "Am I even looking at myself?" I wondered.

I remember seeing friends for the first time after being released. I knocked on one friend's door and when she opened it her face said it all as she let out a small gasp. Eyes big, she said, "Veronica?" as if she wasn't sure. I saw the changes, but I didn't realize that others could see them too.

23

Psychiatwists and Turns

I went to outpatient therapy for big portions of the day for six months. I grappled with my medications and withstood a myriad of side effects.

Dr. R:
"In general, there is the first manic episode followed by a period of not believing the diagnosis is correct, not believing that what happened really happened. A common thread is not taking medication when people start to feel better. It usually takes a few episodes until you see people that take an active management role."

Noelle:
"The meds fucked you up. Lithium. It made you look like you had Parkinson's symptoms. Tremors, forgetful, very cloudy, and lethargic. They didn't do anything for mood because it wasn't a mood stabilizer. You were hesitant to take them because of the way they made you feel. You started getting paranoid that you would get Parkinson's disease."

Dr. E (more on him much later), once said, "We are all different little chemistry sets." Each of us reacts to the same things in different ways. And for myself and Alex, meds come and meds go. They work and then they just don't. While lithium was tough, it kept me in a stable place during the crisis.

Alex B:
"I was on lithium for twelve years. After eight years, I had the four manias, so it had stopped working. I switched to Depakote and Abilify for a while. I recently changed to Lamictal because the other was giving me the shakes and brain fog. You're so blank. I think I still have some of it, but it's not as bad as it was."

Noelle:
"In spite of everything that happened, you were pretty accepting. It went back and forth with meds and with doctors sucking. Psychologists and psychiatrists. They weren't listening to what you were saying or what you needed. They were doing their job and saying they needed to give it time."

I had been out of the hospital for about five to six months and had yet to find the right psychologist, and the relationship with my psychiatrist was not easy either. I just kept trying. I tried until finally I was referred to Dr. R and when I got to her office, I recognized her. She had met me as a newcomer into this strange new place of having a diagnosis like bipolar I. At first, I was inconsistent with therapy as well as medications. In sessions, I would do medication checks for accountability. It took more than a handful of months to get steady on a consistent weekly schedule.

After a while, it was all taking a toll on my relationship with Noelle. I fought hard, and, at times, it felt like Noelle had to fight even harder. This wasn't her first mental health rodeo.

Noelle:
"As the caregiver in a situation like this, I meant well, but there needed to be boundaries. I felt the guilt of asking you if you have been taking your meds. From the caregiver's side, there is a feeling of mistrust. With my ex-boyfriend (who also had bipolar I), if he would start drinking on his meds, I would say, 'Are you sure that is a good idea?' He would get upset. You would feel bad if I asked you too."

Whether it was the side effects, the blunted emotions, the good-natured and well-intended person who says, "Have you tried yoga?" or the fact that I didn't want to have to rely on a pill to keep me functioning, medications were a struggle. It was a terrible cycle that always brought me back to a tiny blue container with seven dividers with the days of the week on them, and a splash of water from the sink. Sometimes as the pills went down, I thought, "Dammit, why haven't I been able to find a way to regulate naturally?" Sometimes, I still have that feeling. To this day, I struggle to take **all** thirty pills every month.

Conversations with my second psychiatrist were very dry and, in retrospect, all but my past two psychiatrists have felt like more than just a vendor of medications. From 2008 to 2023, I had gone through seven psychiatrists. Psychiatrist number two presented as an emotionless man who seemed to only wear brown. One could easily spot him rocking a sweater vest with a button-up underneath. He had a bushy mustache and glasses from what could have very well come from the DMV of 1976.

I was going to Phoenix for my friend's wedding, and when I came back to San Diego, I realized I had left my medications in Phoenix. I notified my sister, Steph, and Noelle to tell them I would call my psychiatrist the next morning. Oddly enough, around 10:00 a.m., he called me instead.

"I'm so glad you called! I was actually going to call today because I left my meds somewhere, and I need to refill my prescription."

When I got to the office, he was quiet at first and almost cold. He then told me, in a stern voice, that my sister and girlfriend had called to tell him what I had done. As if he had caught me in a lie.

My initial reaction inside was anger toward my sister and Noelle. I felt like they couldn't trust or rely on me. Now I'm realizing that they really had to keep matters in their hands, just in case. For months, they were used to doing all the work.

Psychiatrist:
"Because of your actions, I am increasing your Abilify dosage."

Abilify is an antipsychotic medication. It is designed to curb paranoia, hallucinations, depression, and delusions.

This did not make ANY sense. It is not a medication that sharpens memory. With the milligram increase, I was now spending $1,000 a month for thirty pills. As a result of the increase, I started noticing serious side effects. I would fall out of chairs for what seemed like no reason. One time, I was sitting on a stool in my kitchen, drinking coffee, and I slowly fell backward onto my table. I would freeze, and not be able to move when I was out on walks. My speech was slurred, and I would be thinking one word but saying another.

When I read up on Abilify, some of the severe side effects and signs of toxic levels were the inability to control motor movements, loss of balance, and slurred speech. I called my psychiatrist.

"Stop taking it immediately," my psychiatrist said.

How quickly the tables turned.

24

The Difference in a Year

A year had gone by, and time changed a lot of things.

I got two new jobs; one was another music therapy company that primarily worked with kiddos with autism, and the other was a foster school where the teens lived on campus.

I got a new haircut, which truly seemed to change how people viewed and interacted with me; slowly transitioning from long hair, makeup, sometimes high heels, sometimes sundresses, to a fade haircut, no makeup, tailored pants, and button-ups with ties. My internal and external worlds had changed so drastically close together. My mind felt so foreign yet my body, and the way I presented it, had never felt more "me."

The haircut happened right after Noelle and I broke up. This was about a year after the hospitalization. The weight of my mind and moods were part of the eventual fall but it also had to do with my insecurities, and a myriad of other parts that just weren't working.

I really grieved the passing of my relationship with Noelle. I sang my way through the pain and wrote about heartache from what seemed like every angle. Noelle saw me through the biggest moment of my life to that point as a partner, and she did it all at the very start of her twenties. I don't ever remember her frustrations, her pain, her complaints in the midst of my chaos. I don't think that is from blocking it out of my memory. I just don't think she shared that part of her with me.

25

Meet Lindsay

In the midst of healing and dealing, a set of dimples and fancy heels with a big brain for words walked into my life: Lindsay. The only thing I knew of Lindsay was that she was also a musician in the San Diego scene. I quickly realized what a solid lyricist she was. Lindsay is an all-around fight-for-the-underserved type of human. She never met a cookie she didn't like and I don't think I've ever laughed harder with a person.

After a rocky start, Lindsay and I steadied the wheel and started doing life. Before we began our relationship, there was music, music was always first. Songwriting and particularly lyrics were the way we told each other, "I love you" and "You hurt me."

At the start of knowing one another, we would hop on each other's shows with bands we had already established: I would sing on her songs; she would sing on mine. Those vocal harmonies became (some of) our bread and butter. We formed a folk duo called "The Lovebirds" that went six years strong. It outlasted our intimate relationship by almost three years. We used the stage to bring to light our own struggles, in hope others would find some light. I became somewhat of an advocate for bipolar, and she spoke on anxiety and all the panic attacks that come along for the ride.

We sang of our love, of my illness, and how it affected both of us. We even sang about our breakup. After one big manic episode and three full-length albums, we unwound from one another. It was hilarious and tender and awfully beautiful.

I never considered having another episode. I never considered Lindsay seeing me naked in the ways Noelle and my family and other friends had.

26

Going Back for Seconds

On medications? Check.
Going to therapy weekly? Check.
Manic episode anyway? Check.

Lindsay endured the behemoth: the manic episode that drug on. During the first years of our relationship, my manic stories were just that: stories. She had never seen me hit that point, and then she got a healthy dose of it. From the start of this episode on July 5th until mid-October, I was in a fierce battle to find my sanity.

I believe there were a few contributing factors to this break. For one, my medications and doses were not a good fit for me. In fact, one of the medications I was on is known to induce mania.

Secondly, I took on an additional job. This is a common type of trait with someone in the midst of mania. The calendar of events just gets fuller and fuller.

My therapist kept informing me to slow down. I was working in four places, and I was over-the-moon excited for this new position. It was a summer program with teens at a local San Diego high school. I was helping them write musicals. Being in hypomania worked in my favor for a while. I would never have thought I had what it took to accept this job, but in hypomania, no problem, I can do it. Not only can I do it, but I'll also do it better than anyone. I had the charisma, talent, confidence, energy, and desire. I was playing with fire, and it was exciting.

I also found myself doing a lot of creative work. I composed fourteen songs for the different vignettes the teens at the high school wrote in class. I taught all the songs in ten days. It was a high-energy environment, so I just fit right in. Or at least that is how I was viewing things. I also played piano for the performances we had. I worked longer hours and took work home. With my nose down, I was so over-involved I didn't take the time to look up and realize I was in the clouds.

Doing "just one more thing" or sleeping "a little less" can be the tipping point for many people who have a disposition toward extremes. A break is big and loud, but its push into destruction can be so delicate. Tiny things can add up to a lot in a sometimes quick and unpredictable way.

Lindsay:
"You had been working so much with the glee club kiddos. You were so into it, and you talked about the job and the students nonstop. When your brain is in overdrive like that, you are pretty much all output, which, in turn, made me the receiver of sorts. I suspected you were a little unstable because that's usually when I felt the most tired, and I was exhausted during those months."

Lindsay took the brunt of this episode. I'm not sure she knew what she signed up for, but she stuck with me through it all. Even now years later, with a wife and kiddo of her own, she would be there with a light blue or orange Gatorade and chocolate in most forms, telling me everything is going to be okay.

Lindsay:
"When we first started hanging out, I immediately discovered you could shift very quickly between the highs and lows. Then when we started spending more time together, you were much more on the depressed side, which I just felt like I could relate to since I was also at a pretty low point in my life. When we began to date, I really started to observe the differences. You would be very low in the morning, struggling to get out of bed. Other times, you were so energetic that I could hardly keep up. In the very early days of our relationship, medication was not as strict of a routine for you, so it often felt like we were on a tiny roller coaster—nothing too extreme on either end, but definitely much more movement across the spectrum at a quicker rate. I remember feeling very tired in the beginning of our relationship. One particular moment stands out when we were scheduled to play a show with Jeffrey Joe (a friend) at a coffee shop. I told you to drop me off at my house and to play the show without me. I was so exhausted and remembered feeling like I needed a night to decompress."

There were red flags popping up more than a week prior to this break.

Lindsay:
"It was the 4th of July, and I had gone home to visit my family for a couple days. I remember thinking some of your Facebook posts at the time seemed very 'up' but I was too scared to say anything because I didn't want you to think I was jealous that you were having fun without me."

In the past, people in my life had told me they were hesitant to bring things up because they didn't want to hurt my feelings, alarm me, and they weren't sure how I'd react. Now, after some come-to-Jesus moments, pun intended, I encourage my support system to speak up, even if it's scary and unpredictable. I didn't realize I needed to give my whole community the go-ahead, but I have noticed a difference. My behavior and reactions to things seemed to shift how people felt like they could come to me about anything.

When possible, my team is gentle and direct. However, there have been times when matters were taken from my hands when safety was an issue. I understand as a white person that I feel safer calling the cops, and unfortunately I would not recommend getting police involved otherwise. Above all, if my team doesn't feel safe around me in a psychotic state, they need to keep their distance. I am my number one priority, just like everyone else at the end of the day.

When others have open conversations with me about what they are observing while I'm hypomanic, it empowers me by keeping me aware of something that is out of my line of vision. When I don't know I don't know, there is no way I can change things. Open communication also keeps the paranoia at bay. The reality is my team needs to talk about me "behind my back" when they are strategizing in the midst of my mania. The less it feels like that for me, the better. Whatever they can let me in on is appreciated. A "Hey, V, we have been talking with each other because we want to help, just letting you know" goes a long way when I might be getting into paranoia land.

However, if I am "gone" if I am overly confident that I am in fact God and there is no convincing me otherwise, it is best to fool me in the ways I need to be fooled. For example, in mania, I often trust the light and not the dark. If it is apparent I need to be hospitalized, it would be helpful for a friend to say something along the lines of, "Veronica, I know there is some light at the hospital. We could go there and see it." When safety is at stake, it is key to get me to safety, meaning the hospital, by any means possible.

Another discovery that may seem obvious is playing to the manic person's character if they have one. If they believe they are Big Bird, then tell them Sesame Street is near the hospital and that their best friend Snuffy wants them to go there. I would almost treat that state of mania the same way I treat someone with dementia or Alzheimer's—if they live in assisted living and keep asking to go home I don't try to say things like, "You live here, don't be silly." I tell them something like, "Yes, we will be going home, don't worry." Keeping anxiety at a low is key.

It's important for my support system to give me the reigns when I'm strong. It is equally important that they take the reins when I've forgotten how to pull them back.

On July 4th, Lindsay noticed my "unusually high" Facebook post. I must have been noticing some things at this point too because I scheduled a therapy appointment with Dr. R the next day.

Dr. R Notes:
"July 5th, 2011, Med check: Taking as prescribed. Follow up on mood, relationships, and stress (especially related to work schedule). Patient discussed feeling manic euphoria, racing thoughts, difficulty concentrating. Patient discussed how she has been successfully managing symptoms— slowing down, choosing safe, mellow friends to hang out with, taking off work. Developed a plan for next forty-eight hours including seeing the psychiatrist."

During those next forty-eight hours, I was meeting up with Noelle for coffee near my house and I decided to walk there. The closer I got, the more at peace I felt. I was floating in a sea of calm. I felt love surrounding me. The warmth seemed to enrich the vibrant colors the palette of the day had to offer.

I was still Veronica. I was still on earth and alive.

I touched the door to the coffeehouse. I pushed it open and I stepped in.

3... 2... 1... Detonate.

I just stepped into a new dimension. I have died and gone to heaven. In death, it has been revealed to me that heaven is on earth.

Alex B:

"It's common for me to think I'm in the afterlife. I was playing guitar, and I felt like I was falling into some rhythm. A natural flowing. Where I wasn't even doing anything. It was spontaneously happening. I ended up taking off all my clothes, and I peed on the floor and equipment. Then I collapsed on the floor, and I thought I was dead, and it was the afterlife."

I need to confirm that heaven is here.

I approached a man at the coffeehouse. He was a tall, big man who had long dreadlocks. His response fed right into my delusion.

"Is this heaven?"

"Yea, yes, it is."

"Does everyone know it?"

"No, not everyone."

I called my brother, Grant, and asked when he was going to visit San Diego.

He says he is going to try to visit soon. What he is really saying is that he is going to die soon and join me in heaven. My whole family would be dying, and we would all live in Heaven on Earth in San Diego. This is the best news! Heaven is here. Heaven is home.

I'm here! I'm safe! I made it! Not everyone around me is in on the secret.

I remember scanning the coffeehouse slowly.

The people that look back at me are also dead and know. The ones that don't look are still alive. I know I can't ask anyone in case they are still alive and unaware.

Noelle appeared as if from thin air. I forgot she was even coming to see me.

She must know! She came to greet me from Heaven!

Noelle had been here before. She texted Nikki (a friend) and Lindsay:

"Get here! Get here right now."

Noelle:
"Nikki just happened to be close by. I was relieved. I knew I couldn't be the one to ask if you were taking your meds or telling you your thoughts seemed pretty big. I knew I had to go along with everything you were saying until they got there. I was worried you would run again."

    My delusions started pouring out into the world.

Noelle:
"It was starting to go Savior-esque. Like, 'I'm out to save the world.' At that point, you weren't talking about dying to save the world. You just wanted to help everybody. You were talking about God a lot."

    Nikki showed up.
    She knows too!
    I started to explain what was going on.

Nikki:
"V, I don't want to alarm you, but your thoughts seem a little big right now."

    For a split second, I felt alarmed. I took a pause and considered what Nikki said. At this point, my confidence was high and I couldn't be fully convinced.
    Lindsay was at work when she got the text.

Lindsay:
"I know I talked to someone on the phone, but I can't remember much. All I knew was you were in a public place claiming that a coffeehouse was heaven. I just ran out of my office and into my car. I don't even know what I told my boss. I think I was on adrenaline autopilot. I just remember begging God to give me the right words to say to you the whole time I was driving—and then I drove to the wrong fucking coffeehouse like an idiot."

    Lindsay eventually made it to the correct coffeehouse.
    Lindsay! She is dead too! They all came to welcome me.

Noelle:
"When Lindsay got there, she knew what to do. She asked you where your emotions were. You were starting to drift away, but she was still able to get information from you.

"Lindsay drove you to your house. You wanted to get home, and you were getting really emotional. Lindsay texted me, 'Get to the house before we do and hide everything that is sharp.' We booked it back, and Lindsay took a long way. I didn't think that was how you would do it. I was more concerned with your pills. While you were in the car, Lindsay called crying and said, 'Where can I take her?' I told her, and you were yelling, 'I'm not going back to that hospital! I'm not going back to that hospital!'"

I tried so hard to stay "here." I didn't really know what was going on.

Something doesn't feel right. We are driving back to my house. Stay with it, Veronica. You're okay. Don't go over the edge. You don't want to go back to the hospital. It's so beautiful. Something feels terrible. The weight of the world is on my shoulders. This is agonizing. Every s*icide, every sin, every feeling ever felt by every human who has ever lived is coming through me. I can hardly take this. I can't breathe.

Noelle:
"When you got to the house, you seemed like you were on acid, a hallucinogenic drug. It just kept getting worse. Swells of emotions were coming out of you. Real agony and sorrow. It was like someone had died. It was tumultuous."

I am Jesus.

An ensemble of emotions was performing in my head. Then came the paranoia.

Lindsay was trying to give me one of my just-in-case medications to sedate me a bit. *I can't take this pill. Lindsay is trying to kill me. She tells me to trust her, but I know when I take this I'm going to die. I'll spend eternity in hell. Lindsay is begging me and telling me to trust her. She is crying. I beg her to reconsider. A part of me trusts her.* I think I can trust her. *I will take the pill but I know if I do it means there is a good chance I will die.*

I swallowed the pill, and then I threw it up. Maybe my brain was so convinced in this distorted reality I was in that I had a physical reaction. Lindsay got the now-disintegrating pill and gave it to me again.

I was gone. I no longer had the ability to navigate this boat back to the dock and set sail into my next manic episode.

I moonwalked into my next new delusion.

I am Michael Jackson reincarnated. I can't go to the hospital! I have a big tour coming up. Why won't people believe me?!

Lindsay:
"The very first night of your break, I just wanted to make sure you weren't in danger. I kept trying to get you to sleep, or at least stay in bed. You talked nonstop until the wee hours. I think you maybe slept for an hour or two.

"The next morning you seemed a little bit better and I was so relieved for about 2.2 seconds. I think someone brought us bagels. You ate a couple bites, and then you started going right back into the nonstop talking. You kept trying to make spiritual connections out of everything. We had been playing a lot of Mad Libs before all this happened, and you were trying to use them as a code to explain your whole schema about being God. And you kept telling me how I already knew about it too, using the Mad Libs I had filled out as 'proof.' On the outside I was just trying to stay calm, so you would just stay on the couch and talk (even though it was exhausting, at least you weren't agitated or in danger). On the inside, I was freaking out. I didn't know if it was just something we needed to weather or if you needed to go to the hospital. It didn't seem like you were interested in hurting yourself. You were just in nonstop preach/explain mode. Details are fuzzy, but I think that is also the afternoon we went to see the nurse practitioner/psychiatrist. I remember on the way there you were making comments about the music, that you preferred music without lyrics.

"When we got to the building, you saw a mom and a few kiddos in the elevator, and basically sprinted into it so you could interact with them. It was pretty much nonsense, but the mom was not very compassionate—she just went into stranger-danger mode to protect her kids, which was understandable. When we were in the waiting room, you kept trying to talk to everyone else there too. I think it was nothing new to them because they were much more kind and less afraid of you. When we finally got in to see the nurse practitioner, she told me it was her last day before taking sabbatical. She asked you a few questions, and you made absolutely no sense in your responses. She wrote you a new prescription and said it should help you even out within the next couple days. She did not appear to give one flying fuck about you or the situation. I left feeling even more scared. I pretty much had a panic attack on the way back to the car. You weren't very observant of reality, but noticed I was upset and tried to comfort me a little bit.

"The second night was more of the same—I was hell-bent on trying to get you to sleep but you talked incessantly. I think that was the night we called your parents and asked them to come."

My mom and stepdad (Gary) arrived the next day. From my point of view, I was somehow still fighting for my sanity. We stayed close to the hotel they would be staying at. I remember going to a restaurant, and Gary was at the counter in front of us ordering. I had the thought he might be controlling my mom. I was trying to fight the thought but it was strong.

Mom:
"We were eating at a restaurant, and you were kind of loud, so we went outside to eat. You were so very relieved when I said you were not God. You thought you were, and you felt everyone's pain and felt responsible to help them. You would

try to touch people and talk to them to help them."

That night we all went to the hotel. Lindsay and I had our own room. I remember feeling somewhat lucid and hungry. Lindsay and I ordered pizza and had it in our room while Mom and Gary were in their room.

Lindsay:
"We got a room right across the hall from them. I started to have a little hope that you would come back down knowing your mom was close, knowing you were taking this new medication, and knowing that we had A/C in the hotel."

Then the feeling that Gary was controlling Mom came back.

We are in a hotel. I don't know why we are here. I am agitated. I hear something through the wall. It's Gary. He's yelling at my mom!! He's going to hurt her. I am infuriated!!

A rage I had never felt before or since came over me. It surged through my lungs.

Mom:
"You burst into our room (we shared keys) and started yelling at Gary who was taking a nap, mad at him because you could hear him yelling at me. You were angry with him for 'controlling mom,' and described what you had heard him saying to me through the hotel walls. Your eyes were fierce, and you were waving your arms, pointing, shaking your fists. We were both afraid, and the more we tried to quiet you, the more excited you became. Lindsay ran across the hall to get you. She physically removed you from our room, and you strained to get to Gary all the while, yelling at him. It was clear you were trying to protect me."

It wasn't until years after this interview that my mom told me Gary was sleeping when I walked into the room and I jumped on him.

We went back to our room but I don't remember how Lindsay calmed me down. It is possible that my mind went on to the next thing.

Growing up, there was no real reason to fear Gary. He can be a little rough around the edges but he never harmed me. I rarely heard Mom and Gary fight growing up and nothing led me to believe he would treat her poorly in that way. He showed up as a stepparent when he really didn't have to, and he did it starting when I was four years old.

Lindsay:
"You actually slept for a few hours that night, but you woke up in a cold sweat, and begged me to take you to the hospital. You were so paranoid, but nothing you said made sense, so I couldn't tell exactly what you were afraid of."

I can feel what is going on in this hotel. Every person. All of their childhood memories gone wrong, all of their losses, all of their pain. It is all pouring inside of me.

Lindsay:
"I made the decision that we definitely needed to go to the hospital if you were telling me that's what you wanted. I would have never been able to live with myself if I hadn't listened to you, and you ended up hurting yourself. Looking back, I think we should have gone immediately from the coffeehouse to the hospital."

27

Emergency Shmergency

Dr. R Notes:
"Pt was hospitalized on July 9, 2011, due to a manic episode. When staying at a hotel, in room with partner and across the hall from parents who flew in for extra support, Pt requested to go to the ER due to feeling overwhelmed by there being "so many people in this hotel."

Lindsay:
"We waited so long. So. Long. Hours. You were relatively calm for the majority of the wait. Gary waited in the car, and your mom and I were with you in the main waiting area. I asked you so many random questions just to keep you distracted."

    I was sitting and looking around at people. We were in the emergency waiting room. Maybe most of the people were here in search of physical help, but I just needed the stamp of approval to get sent to a place more specialized. I scanned the thin hallway of people waiting to be helped. *Everyone is connected to me and I to them. They are all looking at me and looking to me. Everyone is sick and needs salvation. They need me to save them.*

Lindsay:
"You started getting antsy, so we went outside. I put Otis Redding on my phone, and we slow danced."

I feel like I was searching for an answer in the dark.

"Dance with me, V."

We stepped outside of the hospital into the night.

We faced one another and embraced in time. I felt like I was with her. She was probably freaking out with every cell of her body. But in that moment, I saw Lindsay for the first time in days. The red glow of the emergency sign mixing with the white glow of the moon. Lindsay held her phone up to our ears. Our feet moved together in rhythm and it all seemed to help make everything else make sense. The way music had rescued me so many times in the past, it was here again. I had forgotten about everything for a moment and somehow Lindsay was still there for me, and just as Otis Redding said, "That's how strong my love is." As I calmed down Lindsay was steady, and running on as little sleep as I was, if not less.

Lindsay:
"Eventually, they gave us a little room to wait in, forever. Your mom joined Gary in the car after a while, and they ended up driving back to the hotel to sleep a bit. There was a little old lady in the room, and the staff wasn't being very nice to her. That kind of thing agitated you because you wanted to help everyone. I tried to distract you by asking you to sing with me. Then in walks this random Jesus lady decked out head to toe in Jesus garb. It was so weird. She didn't seem injured, and she didn't appear to be with anyone else. She was just roaming the ER. She talked to us for a little bit, and was very calm and kind and positive. Of course, you loved everything about her. She even made me feel better. She was ushered into some other

room, and that's when you kind of lost your shit."

They are locking her in! She was trying to help me, and now, they are torturing her! Someone help! They are hurting her!!!

Lindsay:
"I basically had to stand in the hall, and yell for someone to help because I didn't know how to keep you calm. There were many times when nurses would just be standing around talking to one another when people needed serious care."

The dam had broken, and Lindsay was standing with a thimble in her hand. She had been dealing with me like this for days on end. On top of that, it was probably around 4:00 a.m. The only thing she could think to do was to sing with me. We sang "Go to Sleep Little Baby" together in the hospital room, and the chattering in my mind faded. The gift of sleep came over me.

Lindsay:
"Finally, they gave you Ativan, and you nodded off, thank God. By the time a doctor came to evaluate you, you were out of it and could barely answer any questions. We waited even longer in yet another room to see if there were any beds open for you. Finally, someone came for you. I was so sad they wouldn't let me go with you because I didn't want you to wake up and wonder where everyone was. I grabbed a pen and wrote on your arm that I would be back the next day. Then I sat on the curb outside the ER as the sun was rising and bawled while I waited for Gary to come pick me up."

I don't remember how I got to my room in the open unit. But I was back again. Thankfully, I wasn't at the hospital I had been at before. This was a little step up, or so I think. I must have been sedated. I wish I had the answer on how to get the best care but a lot of times it's just about Googling the nearest hospital and stepping on the gas.

I was experiencing some paranoia which was clear in my phone call with Dr. R.

Dr. R Notes:
"Pt called (from hospital)—her speech was clear and coherent, but she was vague in content endorsing that she was uncomfortable speaking on the phone. She requested privacy from surrounding others."

I was foggy, but I do remember very well what the unit looked like. A room just big enough for a grand piano. And that is exactly what was in it. It was brown and in tune. I spent a lot of time in that room just letting my fingers get lost on the keys.

There were two main halls. The halls were filled up room after room with patients. There was a big main space with no walls. You could see all the rooms in the halls from that space. Also in the big center space was the nurse's station. It was encased by glass. It seemed the entire staff hung out in there while we were all left to roam in the main space.

Lindsay:
"It was like a ghost town up in there. A desert wasteland. On the open unit, you'd have to hunt all over for someone if you needed staff assistance. Sometimes they would open up an outdoor patio so the patients could exercise. I quickly noticed there was no one monitoring this area. When I actually could find someone, they were some of the rudest and most unhelpful people I've ever met in my life. They could not be bothered to answer any questions. Even though I was scared and exhausted, I really tried in the beginning to be pleasant because you were in their care, and I wanted them to care about you. They talked down to me on a daily basis, and by the end of the experience it was very clear they were not a fan of me, or you, or the love and support you were getting from all your visitors. I went home every day so scared to death you weren't safe. I thought

you might die in there. My head would conjure up all the crazy scenarios that could unfold in a place like that, and it would make me vomit. Each day, the staff's behavior caused me to lose more and more faith. I would cry and pray on my knees every night that something else would watch over you because I knew for a fact the staff was doing no such thing."

I was mostly oblivious to the way the staff were treating us. I vaguely remember a few. Yet, I very clearly remember one who I will call Dr. E. He was the one who really cared about my care. He had long wavy black hair. The kind of hair one might imagine in a shampoo commercial. He had an accent that felt mysteriously far away from where I grew up. His voice was hypnotic and methodical. High cheekbones and a mouth with a curious side smile on it. He was the psychiatrist on staff who then went on to become my psychiatrist for the next decade.

Dr. E:
"Upon meeting you, it was obvious to me that you were presenting with a diagnosis of bipolar disorder, manic phase. It was also clear that while you were intelligent, you were out of your element, and grasping for something to make sense of what was happening to you. Though you did not seem scared, you were anxious and engaging. You were clearly in the 'high' peak of mania."

Up to this hospitalization, my idea of psychiatrists was that they wanted you in and out of their office in five minutes or less. Just enough time to say, "Okay, same time next month?"

My experiences up to this point were all less than ideal when it came to psychiatrists. I never had much of a say in what I might want when it came to meds and sometimes when I was asking for help, I didn't get it from past psychiatrists. To say I struck gold with Dr. E is not an overstatement. It can be hard to find proper support in the mental health arenas. It took me years to find the right mental health team. The important part for me was that I kept looking.

Alex B:
"I have had about three psychiatrists and three psychologists."

I found both my psychologist and psychiatrist at two of the three lowest points of my life. My silver lining.

Dr. E:
"**Psychiatry provides the opportunity to blend science and art into one path. Unfortunately, the art of psychiatry is being lost because of an overemphasis on the simplistic view of life as strictly biological, one view which is in a state of flux. While it may be true that everything is ultimately biological, there is an interplay between environment and biology. I am afraid we are surrendering the art of understanding human beings and their behavior in exchange for a simplistic and lucrative working tool.**

"**We as psychiatrists, are human beings too, and have pain and trauma as well. It is increasingly true that we are less and less likely to see our own reflection before seeing someone else's suffering. There is art in science, and science in art.**"

28

Piano: A Grand Thing to Waste

As fuzzy and medicated as my memory was, the thing that stuck out clearly was the unit's piano. A piano equals home and safety to me. In short, it means Mom. Growing up, I would have sleepovers, and we would sleep under my mom's concert grand piano. That black beauty still stands steady in the music room at my childhood home on the plains of Colorado. It takes up almost an entire room, like the one at this hospital. I remember long childhood winter nights, me staring up from the floor under the belly of that piano, Mom playing whatever her fingers led her to. I always wondered "how does she know how to do that so well?" I still think that when she plays. I know my mother was the biggest influence on the way I play piano. She taught me about dynamics—the louds and softs, the feeling in music. And in life I have taught her about the dynamics of a complex-feeling daughter. It seems from the outside that I got most of the feelings in the family. There weren't enough to go around after me at the age of twenty-five.

I didn't really understand the weight of my mom's piano teachings until after one night of playing songs at a holiday party. When I was finished, my friend said, "Did you grow up Catholic? Because you play like a Catholic."

My mom's experience in learning was much different than mine. Growing up, she had a very strict piano teacher, Dr. Brico. Every week my mom had to come in with a new piece memorized. With every wrong note would be a fresh red-pen mark compliments of Dr. Brico. Marking in time as my mother played each note carefully. Dr. Brico was the first woman to conduct the Metropolitan Opera orchestra, and my mom was her youngest chosen student. I truly believe my mom can play anything on the piano with ease. It's her greatest gift among many great gifts. It's where I see her come most alive, and I love to see my mother most alive.

Growing up I was hooked on the piano, playing at any moment I got before the evening news came on and my music became a "distraction." This "distraction" was a nine-foot concert grande special edition piano. The piano company shipped her the wrong piano, and she refused to send it back. They paid $16,000 for a piano that is now appraised at $265,000. Sitting at that piano feels like I'm sitting at the helm of a great ship, steering it with my fingers as I lean in and lean out. I can read notes but don't really remember being taught how to do so. I know it was my mom though. I would fumble through a book and from the kitchen I would hear my mom shout, "That's a C, not a D!" with her perfect pitch. She can hear any pitch and knows right away what it is just by hearing it—a curse sometimes she admits. If a recording or live performance is even slightly off the pitch, she can hear it, and worse yet, feel it. I know it's bad and out of tune when Mom straightens up her posture.

My fumblings on that piano became fanfares eventually. My fingers stumbled at three years of age until they started gliding around the age of ten across the keys with the confidence to close my eyes and enjoy the music I was creating. If I was angry, tired, excited, anything, I wanted so badly to tell the piano about it. I still cherish the privilege to have that ability.

When I realized the unit I was staying on had a piano, I couldn't get over to it fast enough. When I played I felt connected to "real things." It helped me have feelings and, in the moment, noticeably decreased my paranoia, delusions, and anxiety. Other patients would gather around the piano.

There was an older woman who would sing opera. When my mom came to the unit, she would do the same thing I did—make a B-line for the piano. She made the unit come alive in a way only my mother can. Not only with the light of her smile and laugh, but with her music. She has hands that can reach Rachmaninoff and feeling that came from Liszt and Debussy. My mom is rare in that she is classically trained yet she can also use her ear and heart to play. The mix of that magic is hard to replicate. In the unit, she could accompany anyone on anything they wanted to sing. A skill that took me years of college training to even understand. She only needs to hear a song once before she can mimic it.

There are moments I have the lack of motivation or desire to even look at an instrument, yet the piano is my greatest beacon of light when I can't seem to find the light within me. It's not a surprise to me that music is one of the few things that can light up and activate every lobe in the brain. I wish every person had access to such a way of expression.

29

Sometimes You Get Punched

It was another group time on the unit, and someone was talking though I was not listening. Under the glow of the fluorescent lights, we all worked through whatever it was we were working through at that moment. All the patients were sitting in a circle in the main room. I felt calm and was not talking and from the corner of my eye to my right I saw something moving toward me. I stood up as I turned my gaze toward a woman, a patient, approaching me at a fast-walking pace. *She has a darkness in her eyes.* I remember seeing and sensing. It seemed to hypnotize me. She clenched her fist, and I knew what was next. I quickly took my glasses off, ready for her swing. I didn't even try to protect myself.

I don't remember feeling the pain of it. My response only made her madder.

"Nice right hook."

It really was a good swing, and I wasn't trying to be rude. I was trying to give her a compliment. When you think your God, you give a little more "grace" apparently.

No one reported the incident. My sister just happened to call the next day for an update, and they mentioned it.

I kept giving my glasses away. I gave one pair away to a man who only had one eye. When he put the glasses on, it seemed to mask it. I remember how happy he looked. I wanted to help everyone, the way I must believe God would be, as I *was* God.

30

The Virgin Veronica

Lindsay:
"There was the guy who you thought r*ped you. He was a little too touchy-feely, so that worried me."

I remember him as a tall, slender man with beautiful dark skin and dreadlocks. He was striking to me and felt larger than life. In psychosis, I was convinced that I was pregnant with his twins. I don't know what led me to believe this. At no point in time do I actually recall that he was "overly" affectionate or even made me uncomfortable or got too close.

My sister, Stephanie, flew out for support.

Stephanie:
"Lindsay and I went to the store to get an EPT test to prove you weren't pregnant. They wouldn't let us take it in because they said it might feed into your delusion. We couldn't help but laugh at the fact that we were buying a lesbian EPT tests."

31

The Shot Heard Round the Hospital

The story that seemed to get around to everyone in the hospital. Everyone but me:

I was in my room with my roommate. We were talking, and I was sitting at the foot of the bed she was sitting on. I remember seeing flowers on a table. They were most likely from a visitor of mine. I thought the flowers were from my mother and that she was trying to communicate to me through them. I remember how much love and admiration I felt for my roommate in that moment. The kind of love a daughter might have for her mother.

Lindsay:
"No one would give me a straight answer about anything. I heard about the incident from Stephanie when she called to tell me you had been moved to the ICU. They said there was an investigation, but no one could provide any details. I learned the police had spoken to you and thought it absurd that no one thought it necessary to let me or any of your relatives know that."

All I remember were their uniforms. They seemed tall, and I only remember them from the neck down. I was very disoriented, and I think they were trying to ask me questions.

Lindsay:
"Somehow I pieced together the story that your roommate had accused you of s*xual assault. When I was in the waiting room, already crying after hearing the news, the nurse I hated the most came out (in earshot of other visitors) and assured me with creepy satisfaction that "it definitely happened." Later the social worker told me that no one actually saw anything."

Noelle:
"I couldn't believe the staff. Even the receptionist was awful. I work at the hospital, and I can't imagine any other floor being that rude. There are no other floors that treat you that way. On the other floors, receptionists will walk you to where you need to be. On the behavioral floor we would come in for visitation, and the receptionist would say, 'Oh, another one?'"

If only they knew the reality I was in.

I'm in my room with my roommate. There are flowers on the dresser to my left. My mom is sending me a message through the flowers…wait! My roommate IS my mom. She is visiting through my roommate's body. I'm so glad she is here, I need her.

I scooted closer to her on the bed. I started having loving feelings and felt like reaching out the way a daughter would to her mom.

I may have touched her in a tender way. I'm a lesbian and in this case, it may have made matters worse being she was a woman.

Lindsay:
"After the incident, I was in the waiting room. The woman who accused you was sitting with her family there. She was gabbing about the incident in front of other visitors. The receptionist

knew I was there, but just let her go on. I was afraid I would end her life if I said even one word, plus I wanted to maintain some level of anonymity. The next day, the same situation threatened to unfold, so the receptionist basically outed me to the woman and her family by asking me very loudly who I was going to visit, even though she clearly knew I was there to see you."

I didn't end up interviewing Dr. E for this book until years after this incident. Lindsay never told me about it. So much happened and maybe she felt like it was something I didn't need to carry. I walked into Dr. E's office and pressed record on my phone. We sat, and I let the conversation flow. He was transparent and matter-of-fact. I didn't even know this incident with the woman happened until we dug in for his interview. As he recalled the events surrounding it my mouth hung open. I kept thinking, "This cannot be true. I would never do this." My mind unfolded as the phone kept recording what he was saying, "How many other things happened out of my awareness?" I sat across from him as he brought to my awareness that this incident was much bigger than I could have imagined.

Dr. E:
"Your roommate reported that you sat on her bed and held her hand and then touched her leg. When the incident came to light, the immediate reaction from the hospital was to 'circle the wagons' which only made things feel worse. My natural tendency is to not cover things up and just deal with them when calm has returned. She (your roommate) called the police. It was a big deal in the hospital. It was a huge scandal, in fact, the hospital almost got shut down. The state got involved, and we were all interrogated.

"During my interrogation they had asked me if I thought you had done it and I said, 'no.' Your roommate had a history of accusations. Your case was the impetus for policies and procedures to be set up for these types of cases. Ways to deal with s*xual assault and even in the case of

s*icide. S*xual assault happens on all floors of the hospital; not just the behavioral health unit. It has been twelve years since a s*icide in the behavioral health unit and about a year since a s*icide on another floor in the hospital.

"The nurses had not even documented the incident. In fact, the nurse supervisor got fired after you left. Four others were fired after for lack of documentation."

I asked Dr. E. why things had not been documented.

"Neglect. There is so much neglect in the unit. There are so many times I will come in and ask the nurse about a patient and how they are doing. I came in and asked a nurse, 'How is Veronica doing?' she said, 'I don't think I have met her yet. I have been off for the last three days.' This is a typical response. Even if she had been off, when shifts are switched, nurses are supposed to update each other on the patients. I would ask the nurses if they would take care of a patient in that way if it was their brother or sister and they would say 'no'. This wouldn't change things."

I was glad policies were put into place. It hurt to think I actually made my roommate in the hospital feel threatened or unsafe in any way. She may have been dealing with her own paranoia and delusions. I don't know what she was there for. S*xual assault had been going on for years in the hospital— R*pes, s*icides, and poor documentation, on every floor. Why hadn't these policies and procedures already been put in place? Was it because a patient actually blew the whistle and got authorities involved? Was it because I was a lesbian in a Catholic hospital, and my roommate was female? I only have my viewpoint to speculate from.

Whether to keep space from me and my roommate or because I was getting worse, off to the ICU I went.

Once transferred to the ICU it seems my delusions increased. I remember going back to drinking from what I believed to be the Cup of Truth. This time it was more like the vat of truth. I drank from a pink pitcher they let me have in my room. I would fill it with ice and chew it and chug and chew, and I was freezing.

I remember walking down the hall late one night. There was a bathroom with a sign that said, "Do not enter." I thought I needed to go in there to go to the bathroom. I thought it would be some type of mine shaft when I got there that would send me down. Almost as if it was going to the core of the earth.

A nurse came and got me, and she yelled at me. She got close to my face as if scolding a child.

I remember my room, and I didn't have a roommate. Just my hospital bed table, my pink pitcher of ice-cold truth, a pencil, a ton of paper, and a mind bursting at the seams with psychotic creativity. I was frantically writing and composing, but don't remember what I was writing or composing. I just remember the chaos, filling in dot after dot of eighth notes, quarter notes, measure lines, music.

I would draw five long lines across the page and then start filling it all in with musical notes. I would hum the melodies and rhythms and then write them down as if I were writing a letter to someone. It felt desperate as if I were writing a symphony for someone actively dying. I taped all the paper on the walls.

32

Staff? Hello?

Dr. E:
"Hospitals can be bureaucratic, so changes and adaptation to new demands and needs can be slow and seem unresponsive. I have come to see that for every patient who is admitted or under medical care, whether hospital- or office-based for that matter, there are two patients: the physical patient, and the administrative and electronic records patient. And depending on circumstances, they may be identical or vastly different because the physical patient has one particular set of needs while the other may have a different set of needs, all of which may be regulatory or legal in origin. It is nice when they are a mirror image of the other, but there are times when that is not the case. So, while I do believe regulations are important and necessary, it is often the case that the administrative patient becomes more important than the physical patient because regulatory problems can lead to severe financial losses for hospitals and providers, i.e., losing accreditation by Medicare. My concern comes

from situations when the administrative patient becomes more important than the physical patient."

Punched in the face and no one reported it. S*xual assault scandal and no one told my family—no one even told me. It makes me wonder what else goes left unsaid.

Dr. E.
"The reason things were getting overlooked so much was because the hospital couldn't afford to fire nurses."

In retrospect, I'm glad I was being medicated so heavily.

Lindsay:
"During one visit you were eating mashed potatoes and fell asleep with the spoon mid-bite."

I'm glad I didn't notice the absence of staff. The lack of care. The way staff treated the most "out-of-it" patients like animals. And the meds made me tired, but they also softened the blow for a lot of my stay.

33

Visitation Vignette

Jeffrey Joe (a friend/visitor):
"You showed me a crayon drawing you'd made of a house, a tree, some family members, and Jesus."

'See? There's a cross, John the Baptist, Mary…'

"You pointed to the cross and whispered, *'That's me. I am Jesus. I know he's dead. So, I have to be dead in order to set things straight again.'* Lindsay had to leave a couple times to break down out of sight…The room was raucous and noisy with folks walking around and talking loudly and a verbal skirmish broke out over the TV's volume."

Lindsay came back into the room—she always came back.

Lindsay:
"There was a teenage kid who kept telling his parents to bring him condoms, which I found worrisome. Another woman in the ICU had a lot of dangerous outbursts where they would have to lock down the tiny unit until they got her under control. One time that happened and they wouldn't let us leave the little TV room. I remember being scared but glad that visiting

hours were essentially extended because of her."
Some faces were familiar.

Lindsay:
"There was a lady who I recognized from when I worked the food line at Father Joe's (an organization that helps people living in tents/outdoors) a few months prior."

Out of all the patients, I had the most visitors—a common theme that now after two hospital visits seemed to hit me in a more serious way. I wasn't thinking about how my friends and family were worried when they left me after each visit. I didn't know it was affecting them too. It was this hospital stay that made me notice my worth to those around me and the effect a person can have. Both positive and negative.

I never realized that just below me a few floors down were all of my people rooting for me.

Jeffrey Joe:
"A big group of people gathered at the chapel that was downstairs in the hospital. Everyone was a soft blue from the colored chapel windows. Allegra (a friend) was there singing and playing. We all sang 'What a Wonderful World' and I think I played 'Stardust.' There were a few prayers made aloud; The Lord's Prayer, a couple anecdotes about you and most of us were crying pretty hard. I drove home in a rage, crying hard and shouting at the universe."

Christine:
"It was so sad but so powerful. All of these people came to the chapel. They knew they couldn't see you, but they just wanted to be there. There were probably twenty to thirty people."

I read back on this moment from the chapel when I need to remember how many people love me and that I'm not alone. Even through all of this, I need reminders from time to time.

Kristen (a friend/visitor):
"I went to visit you in the hospital, and I remember your flat affect. You wanted to lead a drum circle with the other patients. I was in the hangout room, and you were trying to gather everyone around. You were still having your own struggles. You weren't yourself. But there was a glimpse of you. There was another guy there, a tough military guy, and he was opening up to you and talking about his struggle. You were standing next to him and listening to him. Even though you were having your own struggle, there was still that piece of you that made people feel safe. He was in there because he would black out. He had PTSD. He would get violent, and not remember that he would be hurting people he cared about. You had your hand on his shoulder.

"You asked him to be a part of the drum circle. He didn't want to join, but you told him he could just watch. I could tell he was in pain. The other guy in the group was on the spectrum (autism spectrum disorder). He wanted to be a part of the drum circle, but his rhythm was off. You kept asking him to follow. 'Pat, pat, clap clap, pat, pat, clap, clap.' Then you had people add things. He couldn't get the rhythm. You kept stopping the drum circle. You finally said very sweetly, 'You know, maybe you can sit this one out.'

"You just wanted to care for people. It was heartbreaking. I left there crying. I was crying because you were so sweet and tender with the other patients, but it was also that you were so gone..."

I really wanted to believe what others were telling me.

Christine:
"It was Pride weekend. A Saturday. After the parade, we came to see you. It was a San Diego bright summer day. We went outside. We were bouncing the basketball. You kept asking me if there was a storm coming from the ocean. I kept telling you it was sunny. You kept saying, *'Are you sure?'*"

I was also getting to a space where I wanted to "look normal" to the staff so I could leave.

Lindsay:
"You kept asking me to bring you a suit because: 'Look good, feel good.'"

I wasn't feeling so good and thought it would help. I also wanted to seem more put together, so others would believe I was of sound mind. I was still very much gone at this stage.

34

If I Could Turn Back Time

Dr. E told me if I could memorize the months of the year backward, he would release me. Sounds simple, but for some reason, my brain just couldn't do it. I spent time each day trying to memorize them. I couldn't figure it out. It felt like he came in day after day, and I just couldn't get it.

Lightbulb.

I drew images next to each month. December had a Christmas tree; August was a picture of my little sister, Theresa, because that is when her birthday is. My brain works in such a different way when I'm in mania. It's like parts of it are broken while other parts are let out of the cage.

Having a music therapy background was very useful in this moment. I drew five lines for a musical staff, then started writing the melody to my backward month song. I started with December and came up with an easy little tune to remember it better. After completing the song, I sang it over and over again, rehearsing it like I would for a show.

Finally, the day came when he entered the room and asked me to recite the months. I stood up and started marching in place. It helped me keep rhythm with myself and to keep the song on pace. I started sweating and felt flush in the face. I thought, *"If I can only do this I can get out of here."* And then I sang it back to him, concentrating the whole time.

"And Januaaaaryyyyyyyyy."

Dr. E knew I had a massive support unit and took a chance. Looking back, had Dr. R been involved and had she been allowed to make the call, I would have probably been in the hospital for another handful of days with outpatient required. But Dr. E gave me his word and kept it.

Dr. E:
"You did not seem afraid, nor were you intrusive during our interview. You were able to take my directions very well and were agreeable. After our interview, I felt that all would go smoothly, based on my prior experience. I thought it would be just a week or so and then you'd be back home."

What my network of people (and I) didn't know was how much locked doors helped. We didn't know how much work my partner and friends were going to have to do or how much the people in my life were going to be worried while having to live their lives at the same time. I didn't think about the lives of others during months and months of recovery. I was just surviving.

I wasn't even able to successfully fill out my release papers, and staff said I was nowhere near ready to be released. In fact, at the bottom of the page where it said, "Signature," I wrote "God" in cursive.

I did not go to outpatient therapy after this episode. The combination of early release and lack of outpatient therapy made for a long recovery. This became the everlasting gobstopper of episodes. It damaged my relationships in different ways. Especially my relationship with Lindsay, the person I was closest with.

Dr. R:
"I have a feeling that if you had been working with Dr. E before getting admitted into the hospital, he wouldn't have suggested releasing you. I know he didn't know where your baseline was. He was going with what you would expect someone's baseline to be given the severity of your symptoms. You were in a space where people outside could keep you safe so he released you. You weren't yet stable on your meds. Your mood was really flat. Very dissociated. And I remember we met soon after and Lindsay was with you. It probably would have been good for you to stay in the hospital a bit longer. Dr. E and I had a conversation about your baseline. He had never met you and had no idea but was receptive. But at that point, he said, "It's possible she might not get back to her baseline," but in the past, you had and I knew you would get back to it…

"'The Plan' (more on this later) we put together was in place to keep you safe. You were never left alone outside of the hospital. This was such a gray area for everyone involved. You want people to be in the least restrictive setting, which for many is at home."

In retrospect, the hospital was the least restrictive setting during my second episode due to early release. There are a lot more opportunities for distraction in the outside world. Everything feels a lot faster, brighter, spicier, too much.

The moment I walked out of the doors of that hospital it felt like the exotic zoo animals were released, and I knew I wasn't ready. The only thing I can try to compare it to is how someone in the middle stages of Alzheimer's might feel: You are aware your brain isn't functioning, but you can't stop it. Partially in reality, but partially living somewhere else. No one could have prepared me for this. Night after night after night after night, my psychosis made sure the wild things came out to play. I thought I would hear people under my bed and could swear someone's mouth was right by my ear. I would keep my eyes closed and pray to whoever would listen that it would go away. Meanwhile, Lindsay was still going to work and trying to juggle it all. I don't know how she managed. And I wonder what long-lasting damage I have caused her even to this day.

Lindsay:
"It was grueling. You were still highly delusional and paranoid. I was so happy to have you home, but wondered every day if it was a mistake. We would make the tiniest steps forward, and the next day it would be like some cruel Etch A Sketch in your brain shook everything up and put us back at square one. It was so disheartening. I had a very real concern you were not going to get better. Every little thing scared you, and you had absolutely zero confidence in yourself. I seriously contemplated the idea of us moving to Colorado so you could be home with family because I didn't know how much longer I could do it on my own. I remember I kept trying to fix all your doubts about everything, so you could see you were still capable. You would have excuses for everything because you were so afraid. You couldn't compose or work without the right equipment, so I bought an extra laptop on Craigslist and an amp. You were afraid about not finding work, so I helped you make one resume for music therapy gigs, one resume for coffee shop gigs, and flyers for music lessons. You were afraid about not passing your certification test, so I tried to help you gather all the materials you needed to study. I knew deep down, no matter how much crap I bought or how hard I worked on a project for you, it would all be pointless until you really started to find that confidence in yourself. But I was also flailing and feeling so helpless—doing shit like that made me feel not so out of control."

I wanted to be normal and do normal things. I couldn't find it anywhere.

Kristen (a friend):
"We went to get tattoos, and you were not in a good place. My sister saw you and started crying. You were so sensitive to the thought that everyone was talking about you. You were really adamant about getting a tattoo."

I remember taking a sharpie at the tattoo place and writing the words "Be Love" starting from my wrist to my forearms. It was in shaky handwriting because of the medications.

It reminds me of the nails in Jesus' hands. I am Jesus—I need this tattoo.

My friends alerted the tattoo artist about what was going on so I did not get the tattoo.

Hallucinations, a rarity for me, were starting to bubble up, too.

Kristen:
"We were trying to get you out of the house a little bit at a time. Fresh air, community. One day I said, 'Hey, you want to walk with me to 7-Eleven and get an iced decaf coffee?' You said 'Yes.' You had been out for a week or two by this point. It was sad because I felt like you should have been better by then, and more than what you were."

This was the first break Kristen had witnessed.

"When you were walking, you were uncomfortable and stiff. Timid. You were trying to be normal and talk, and you would apologize all the time. When we got to where we could see the 7-Eleven, there were some people outside. You were really uncomfortable and you said, 'Kristen, did you see that? Did you hear that?!' I said, 'No.' You said, 'That guy whispered in my ear. He whispered, 'Spiders!' I remember saying, 'Oh yeah? I didn't hear it.' I didn't want to feed into your delusion, but I didn't want to tell you that you were just hearing things…

"Later that night Lindsay sent a 911 text saying to please come to the house because she needed support with you. I had to work, so I couldn't come. Molly called me and said that you just wanted to talk to me, so I came. I told my job it was an emergency. I called Molly. She said you didn't want anyone near you. You were sitting on the corner of Florida and El Cajon on the street. You were walking away, and you were really upset. Molly was watching you from far away. I drove and parked and saw you sitting on the corner. You were so angry. You were pacing and telling me how angry you were. You were stomping your feet. Very animated. You wanted to cry. You yelled, 'I JUST WANT TO FEEL SOMETHING!' You decided to walk back to the house with me. We got to your house, and several friends were there. You walked into the house, and you were angry and kept yelling, 'I'M SO ANGRY!' We kept telling you it was safe to let it out. You kept saying it couldn't come out. We decided to try and help you let it out. We all went to the bedroom and stood around the bed and started yelling, and we were all hitting the bed to try and get you to do it. You finally joined. You were punching the bed and finally, you cried."

I felt so out of control and so blank inside at the same time. Anger has always scared me. I don't like seeming angry, jealous, or out of control. But to watch it from the outside, I'm sure it can seem bizarre and frightening. I've been known to hit myself repeatedly and verbally abuse myself. I think part of the reason I turn the anger toward myself is I don't want to turn it toward anything else. A wall, glass, or so much worse, another person.

I was doing what I could to get my feelings out. It was both helpful and hard to go to therapy with Dr. R. Getting out of the house was tricky, and there were delusions and paranoia aplenty. Once there, I felt I could trust her. Her room was simple. White walls, couch for me, chair for her. It helped having such a simple scape to look at. There wasn't a lot to misinterpret. I listened to her. I listened so intently because I thought I was God, and she was my father. I believed she was my God, who I answered to and honored.

This was around the time the delusion that men were controlling everything started happening. When I was in the waiting area for therapy, one of the lights kept flickering on and off. If there was a man present, and the light flickered off, I thought it was because he was controlling it.

He is showing me who the boss is, and, as a reminder, is messing with my head.

I had a similar delusion about myself. When I saw music videos Lindsay and I had done, I couldn't get through watching them. I kept thinking I was controlling her with my eyes every time I looked at her in the video.

Dr. E was another key figure in my religiously themed delusions. The script got flipped once I left the hospital. While I was in the hospital, I confided in him but now I had a hard time trusting him. I had a hard time being in the same room as him. This might be solely because he is a man. I had put my mental health team into extreme corners—I thought Dr. R, a woman, was the highest God. I thought Dr. E, a man, was now Satan or a demon. I have this image left in my head of him in his chair blinking his eyes. His eyelids appeared to shut from left to right—much like a reptile.

My ability to trust him rode on one thing: Was he or was he not wearing glasses?

If I came in and he was wearing glasses, I felt like I could trust him. In my mind, there was a barrier he was creating. *Now he can't steal my soul through my eyes.*

I hated cracking the door open and seeing him seated in his chair with his legs crossed and hands folded with no glasses on. In reality, he was trying to bring me back. We would do math problems backward, recite the alphabet backward, anything to jumpstart my brain. It really felt impossible. I had a brain game book at home; Lindsay would quiz me. Dr. R assured Dr. E that I was a lucid, vibrant member of society. As time passed, he may have wondered.

35

Coming Up for Air

I ping-ponged from one mental health team meeting to the other.

Dr. R Notes:
"August 2, 2011, Blunted affect and tearful. Slow speech. Some delusions about the ocean."

"August 3, 2011, Follow up on mood and delusions, safety, etc. Continued to reinforce temporary nature of symptoms and use of support system. Pt's speech is less slurred/slow. Thoughts surround control and concern about being connected to others."

I was switching back and forth between lucid and the house of someone who had lost their mind. During my moments of sanity, I would write reminders on paper and tape them to surfaces—floors, walls, doors—anything to remind me I would be okay. On the door, I wrote a note that said, "No one is going to kill you. You can go outside."

I'm sure the house looked like a madhouse with all the papers. In my quest for balance and sanity, I ironically created a space that ended up looking like a lunatic's house, but the notes did help.

It was around this time Lindsay felt it would be a good idea to get out of the house. She rented out a place right next to the ocean.

Having the privilege of access to financial resources was the only reason I was able to rehabilitate the way I did. I'm not sure how people do this without. I would have easily burned through my own savings in just a few weeks.

One night, a group of my friends came to visit. I tried to lead a drum circle with the kitchen utensils and appliances in the house and I circled everyone up. Some people on the couch and some on the floor. Everyone started banging on things and almost immediately, it ended up being too much. I got angry and overwhelmed and everyone left. I remember curling up on the kitchen mat, paralyzed by fear, unmovable.

I could hear the waves from the house, which ultimately made the time at the ocean house difficult. Lindsay was doing her best, but we didn't realize a recurring delusion would revolve around the ocean. Christine, Lindsay, and I went out to the shoreline, and I went into the waves, which I believed would be the last time.

I don't remember it being cold, but it felt windy that day and as my body fell deeper into the water, my face was getting splashed. I could no longer feel the earth beneath me physically or mentally. I couldn't catch my breath and felt excited and panicked. I let the wave hit me and went under. *Stay under.* But somehow, my lungs led me back to the surface. *You have to save the people of the world.* Every time I would go under, the physical part of me would save myself. My mind was convinced of what I had to do but my body refused. *It's the only way, Veronica. Sacrifice your one life for everyone.*

Christine and Lindsay did not come in to rescue me. To them, it just looked like I was being swept under and coming back up through each wave. Every time I went under the voice "stay under" would yell while the other piece of me that loves life, the lucid part of me, begged it not to be so.

36

O Brother, Where Art I?

Lindsay was worn completely thin. My older brother, Brandon, came out to watch me. It was a pretty good fit at the time because Brandon is very steady, logical, to the point, and always seems to have a handle on situations.

I remember drawing a picture of him. Even in my back-and-forth fragile state, I remember thinking, "Why doesn't this look like him?" It was distorted and looked like a children's drawing. I sharpened my colored pencils and colored it all in, confused.

When I tried to write lyrics to songs, my handwriting was different too. My mind was informing and changing many parts of me.

I remember Brandon was very interested in the streets in San Diego. He wanted to know where the doctor's office was, in what little neighborhood, by what types of shops. He might have been making small talk. Maybe he was acclimating himself or just trying to make conversation with the shell of who he once knew me as.

He is devising an evil plan, though I'm not sure what it is…

I was very nervous and paranoid to be in the car, let alone drive, and Brandon had to take me everywhere. I didn't think I'd ever be able to get behind the wheel again myself. Everything seemed so fast as my mind with meds made me feel so confused. I kept missing each target, each social cue, I wasn't back yet.

37

Camera One, Camera Two

About a month passed outside of the hospital.

Dr. R Notes:
"**August 9, 2011, Follow up on mood, safety, delusions, and concerns about control. She continues to have paranoia about "People are coming to get me" and issues of control. Slow movement. Slow speech but occasional positive affect.**"

Lindsay and I went home from the beach house. It didn't matter where we would go because nowhere felt safe.

When the sun left, an eerie feeling came over me, like a shadow on a moonlit grave—my grave. The one thing scarier than night in a psych ward in the midst of delusion is night in the world in the midst of delusion because there are not as many boundaries. I would frequently get up in a panic and look around my room. *Something is in here.* My bedroom window faced the sidewalk, which made matters worse. I would hear people pass, and every time I did, I thought they were all passing, and then sneaking close up to my house, waiting, trying to find a way in. This lasted for months on end.

Episode one and two had a lot of differences but there were certainly through lines in terms of what types of psychosis I had from the first episode to the second.

Noelle:
"The first episode you didn't talk about the delusions, but the second, you were telling us the delusions like you were just talking about any topic."

I think this is due to the fact that I didn't even know what a delusion was when I was experiencing it the first time. I was able to give it a name in the second because I had been here before.

Noelle:
"In the first, you seemed angry and caught off guard. Very abrupt, like a switch had flipped, and the second one was more grandiose. You seemed more cognitively aware of what you were thinking and everything seemed more detailed. There were more layers and details to the delusions. I think the biggest difference was that the first was by such surprise, and that influenced it for all of us."

The duration was also very different.

Christine:
"The first one, you started to recover, but you never came back to the original Veronica. The one image that sticks with me is the super excitable, big plans, big ideas, crazy, shaking your leg, and lying on the ground on stage at your shows. None of that came back. It was like you came into your body a little more."

There were some similarities.

Noelle:
"In both episodes, you were feeling like you had to be a martyr. Having to die to save the world."

There was some silver lining.

Christine:

"In the second there was some relief because we knew you would be coming back. That break felt a little more like you and not so much like this other being as in the first. In the first you were convinced that you were God and believed in all of your delusions. In the second, it felt like you knew you were delusional, but you still had to validate things. You didn't really know if it was real or not."

38

Take Me to Church

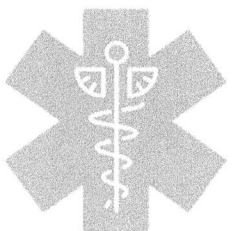

I remember how gloomy the weather was around that time. I could never see the blue skies. It was like the May gray of San Diego, but we were in the midst of summer. I actually thought I was in some sort of snow globe and felt trapped.

Dr. R Notes:
"August 16, 2011, Follow up. Taking meds as prescribed. Pt reports depressed mood with congruent affect."

I was experiencing the dark sides of mania along with depression. Manic agitations, the disorientation, the sudden motor movements, the tears. It was as if a barrel of melted tar was being poured on top of me. I needed hope, and so I went back to my old way of thinking, the old things that used to work for me as a child: Catholic Church.

This is always toeing a line—if I'm asking to go to church, there is usually some piece of me that is delusional. In my day-to-day lucid form, I do not affiliate with religions. I decided to go with my sister, Stephanie. I remember the priest's eyes, and I felt like he was staring into me.

He knows I'm God, and he is a demon spitting hate.
After church, I went for coffee and donuts.
Everyone here is a demon, and they all want something from me.

I felt like I was remaining calm physically through it all, but I felt like I was on high alert.

39

The Med Game

I was taking medications consistently all because of Lindsay. It was not because I didn't want to take mediation. I just couldn't remember to do it on my own all the time. Lindsay had written a list of my medications on a paper and hung it in the bathroom, and she would help out in moments of forgetfulness. I feel like I had more resistance with Noelle telling me to take my meds. I needed Lindsay to take care of that detail.

Dr. R Notes:
"August 23, 2011, Planned a schedule for next two days and discussed the benefits of scheduling her days. Provided a list of pleasant activities. Pt said MD took her off lithium. Pt said that, "I feel really down…unmotivated."

Dr. E was crucial in this game of chemical strategy. He had me on six medications. It wasn't easy, but with one full episode under my belt I knew what could happen. I shook so hard I couldn't interact with music, I couldn't write songs because I couldn't grasp a pen without dropping it. I couldn't play my guitar because my fingers would dance all over the fretboard from the shakes. When I tried to sing, my voice shook and if I held out any long notes, the shakes were audible. I could feel and hear the pulse of my heartbeat anytime I held out the notes quietly. Even though I had "been here" before, there was a fear that my abilities as a musician wouldn't ever come back.

Take 2.5 mg of this, get off of that, start this medication at 5 mg, two months later bring it up to 10 mg, introduce this, lower that, get off of that, lower this, get back on this for two weeks, and then let's see where to go from there. It takes something special to keep going on a cocktail of meds, for me, especially in the beginning of a crisis.

Time passed and so did the psychosis. In the words of my friend, Jeffrey Joe, "TTT": time takes time. The paranoia, delusion, and hallucination left the party eventually, and shortly after, a very deep depression wanted in. My episodes have thus far been followed by a hefty depression.

40

We're All Just Cakes

On a podcast about mental health, an interviewer asked me, "When is it bipolar and when are you just being a jerk?" I think at the time the answer was as poignant as, "I don't know." Had I been able to put thought into the response I might have said, "That feels like asking someone, 'what part of this cake is flour?'"

It may be impossible to separate in my mind.

41

For Better or Worse, Repeat

Dr. R Notes:
"September 6, 2011, Pt discussed low motivation and confidence.

"September 13, 2011, Pt was tearful and reported feeling depressed.

"September 27, 2011, Pt discussed life being chaotic. Pt discussed feeling more like herself but being tearful still."

Lindsay:
"There were all these tiny little triumphs that kept hope alive. I would see little glimmers of the real you and that would fill me back up."

I think about this idea of the "real me." It's hard to say who that is with each passing day given the biggest events in my life that have occurred without the consent of my own mind. I've noticed the further I get from an episode the more I tend to "forget" I have bipolar. That's when I have more conviction that, "Oh, this is the real me." It is in the moments that I seem to lose it in anger or emotion that I point to the bipolar, but I don't know if that's always true or fair.

Dr. R Notes:
"October 4, 2011, Pt reported improving mood."
In true form to my diagnosis, I was riding the pendulum.
"October 18, 2011, Pt discussed feeling less motivated and "lost." She discussed feeling like her life is in a holding pattern."
It was around this time my music therapy boss requested I record a children's song about handwriting. My lack of confidence made it difficult. I remember going into the office with Lindsay, she kept trying to help, and over and over, I would say, "I can't do it. I can't do it. I can't do it." It must have been one too many "I can't do it." In frustration, Lindsay grabbed the headphones used for recording and threw them to the ground. It was the first and only time I remember Lindsay getting frustrated with me.

Lindsay:
"It was the first time I had ever seen you not confident about your musical abilities. Which was jarring. Even in the hospital, you were a confident musician. To watch you have overwhelming insecurity was a completely different thing. I think the times I lost my cool in front of you were not many. I would save that for later so I could process it when I wasn't with you. Like screaming in my car. I remember I slammed a mirror down and it broke. I would think we were getting somewhere, and then it was just like the movie "Groundhog Day." The nighttime brought it. So many weeks of nonlinear healing. Over time it got better and better but it was not a straight line from point A to point B.

"I remember the frustration of knowing you needed space from me. I needed it too. But I was keeping you safe. I couldn't just leave you. I don't think you understood that. You thought you were better than you were. You would tell me you didn't want me around you. It hurt my feelings but, on a level, I needed the same but no one was there to take over fully."

Dr. R Notes:
"November 1, 2011, Pt discussed that she will start studying for her recertification exam.

"November 15, 2011, Pt is attempting to give ten guitar lessons a week and looking for a coffee shop job."

Lindsay:
"The fog finally just started to lift after a few months. It felt like forever, but looking back now I think it was pretty freaking impressive that you were able to pass your board certification test and get the coffee shop job, and that we started playing shows as early as October."

It could have been me adjusting to meds better, or that some time had passed, or that I had such a good group of support around me. But I believe the fog lifted because of all the moving parts and not just one thing.

As more time passed, I was becoming more and more like myself. The lesson of episode two? Best for me to fully recover in a controlled environment and to seek aftercare.

The sweltering summer of my nightmares was over. Fall was touch and go. Winter came, and the year changed. The year anniversary of this break was steadily getting closer.

I was working at my second music therapy position with the same type of population (mainly Autism Spectrum Disorder) when I had my second manic episode. It was awful feeling like I would never be able to handle working there again. I lost my first music therapy job because of a manic episode, and I really started to believe this was going to be the story of my life: Build a wonderful life for myself, watch it grow, have an episode, everything is gone, sit in a long dead space of time, crawl back into the workforce, slowly relearn everything, start feeling real in life again, start doing really well, build a wonderful life for myself, watch it grow, have an episode…

There were days I had to last-minute cancel on clients because I was feeling too paranoid to come into work, because I couldn't get out of bed, because I was running on high, because I couldn't focus. But contrary to past experience, my boss believed in me and didn't give up.

Having one person in the working world believe in me, despite obvious setbacks, was a big thing that propelled me back into putting value on the work I did again. It made me feel like I was valuable. My boss, Michelle, was able to dissolve a fear I had, a fear some people with a diagnosis may have: If people know I'm schizophrenic, bipolar, depressed etc., then they won't hire me. They will give up on me. They will not believe me.

42

Real Joy

About a year out, I had healed some. From the outside, it seemed I had just gotten "back to normal" with steady jobs, steady performing, Lindsay and I had some moments to laugh and breathe. I just wanted to be pre-twenty-five-year-old Veronica. I wanted to be the Veronica who wasn't aware of all the scary things.

Dr. R Notes:
"January 25, 2012, Pt discussed dissociative symptoms."
I kept leaving my body and sometimes I felt like a floating pair of eyes or like I was looking through a lens into another world but it was actually the world I was walking in.

A month before the anniversary of the break, I was having four- to five-second delusions on a regular basis. My therapist noted I had pressured speech, and I needed to slow down. I was getting used to living in my madness on a pretty consistent basis.

In the words of my stepfather, "If you keep doing what you're doing, you'll keep getting what you're getting." While working my music therapy job, I made the choice to take a lead role as a music director for a musical which was an additional one-day-a-week commitment as the cherry on top.

I went back to the things that started my last episode. This was in no way intentional. It's just what my patterns led me back to. Doing, being, working, playing, everything adding up slowly.

Dr. R Notes:
"September 18, 2012, Pt discussed feeling anxious and overextended this week due to two one-day jobs she took on."

By December, my psychiatrist had to increase one of my medications.

In reviewing the notes, some of the biggest blips were surrounded by the fact I wasn't consistent with medications.

Dr. R Notes:
"Pt Speech was a bit rapid. Hasn't been taking medication regularly. Some overconfidence."

For years, I was stopping and starting medication. Med consistency was a struggle. I had all sorts of reasons to not take them. I said it stifled my creativity, I didn't think I could live with the side effects, and the prices of meds that didn't have a generic brand yet. Deep down there's always been the knowledge I can't live as clearly without them. And in my case and in some other cases, medication can be life or death. I've probably been on fifteen to twenty different medication combinations in the span of my diagnosis, which at this point is fifteen years. I've lied about taking them, I've told the truth about not taking them, I've taken them every other day to save money, I've taken them only when I'm not feeling too tired or unmotivated to get up and do it. None of that compares to consistency. In talking with my friends who have different types of mental illness diagnoses, this is an occurrence that seems to be human. Not wanting to be different, not wanting to feel weak, when the reality is, seeking help and taking meds takes mega guts.

Alex:
"Some nights I skip but it's been pretty consistent for years. Lithium every day for eight years. The brain fog really sucks. People are talking but the words aren't being translated into things I can understand. The only thing you can do is say, 'Yeah.'"

As of 2023, Alex is on Lamictal and Abilify. I have also been on those medications.

Alex:
"I think it's better to be on one or two meds at a time. More than that, and I don't know. It seems like too much to figure out."

I want to experience my joy. In order to experience joy, I have to let go of my desire for the high. A manic high is an explosion—beautiful in the moment, damaging in the aftermath. Real joy happens when I can deepen relationships; when I can work toward my life goals, and come up with new ways to serve others. That's where I can find my personal power.

43

Mom, Dad, I'm Gay...and Cray

I know part of the reason it was easier for me to "come out" about my diagnosis is because I had previous experience, "coming out." Plus, it happened so suddenly and everyone was there to witness it. Initially, realizing I was queer was equal parts a sigh of relief and frightening. I thought people would judge me, walk away from me, and possibly disown me. While that may have been the case for a small percentage, I was luckily incorrect for the most part. It felt like when I was told, "You have bipolar I" I was in shock but it felt like a good explanation for what I had been experiencing. Having bipolar I puts a strain on myself and my relationships, but no one in my life has walked away solely because of it.

My life and the way I want to live it is dependent on my medication. It's dependent on my therapy: leaving the party early if I didn't sleep much the night before, speaking up when I'm feeling off, removing myself from triggering environments, reaching out, and checking in with myself. And for me, it isn't a perfect road. At 40 I'm still finding that days can go by where

I forget to take meds or feel low so I don't get up to get them. I know what works and still I don't always do it.

It seems for some that taking medications and going to therapy are signs of weakness, whereas independence is seen as a sign of strength. From my experiences, the reality seems to be the exact opposite. It takes courage to seek help. It is bold to break ground on the journey that is medication and it is important for many to live in community.

I know medication is not the be-all and end-all. Many people with bipolar can lead a stable life without medications. There have to be other stabilizers put in place specific to each person. It has been clear I'm not one of those people at this time in my life. I have consulted with my mental health team and they strongly agree with one another—medications will allow me to live my life more consistently.

When I had my second clubfoot surgery at twelve, I remember people being careful around me, and they were comfortable asking me how I was doing. They would ask if there was anything they could do for me. It was okay that I needed medication to get through the physical pain, but having a nervous breakdown during the Monday morning meeting, it might be that work associates talked about me in a quiet voice. Maybe out of concern, maybe out of being uncomfortable, or maybe to poke fun because it's too close to home or too unknown.

The other side of this coin is when people can see pain, they don't have to be told to help. Many people struggle from the inside, and nobody knows it is happening. The questions I've asked in my head at times being, "How is it that they can't see that I'm suffering?"

44

The Plan

It was important for me to acquire tools in prevention and preparation for disaster. My therapist told me it would be a good idea to make a box of good memories. Inside are pictures of friends that make me feel safe when I'm manic, cards that are special to me, a poem my sister, Theresa, wrote when she was ten years old that I love, and a letter to Manic Veronica. The purpose of the box and its contents are to convince me to come back down if I am manic.

The most valuable tool for my support system is something Dr. R and I developed called, "The Plan." It was designed in case I don't have the mind to tell people which hospital to take me to, or who to call. It also details how my own mania comes on in phases. At the end of this book there is a QR code that will give you access to a template of The Plan. Just use your phone's camera to access it by hovering over the QR code. Don't actually take a picture of the QR code, it will come up as a yellow link that you then click on. This is useful for anyone—not just people with mental illness. Not every person with bipolar does have the same trajectory, but I found it very useful to write things down in retrospect. For me, builds into mania have all looked somewhat similar.

I will be leaving out personal info like phone numbers. The following is MY Plan but the link will let you tailor your plan. I think if you are or you know someone with bipolar or other mental illnesses that result in episodes, this is a good tool to bring into your toolbox.

The Plan

CODE WORD if you think I'm manic is **"cantaloupe."** I use a code word so it's easier and quicker to bring up to me. I cannot tell when I'm manic. If it's at the beginning of hypo(low)mania then I will proceed by asking what types of symptoms you have noticed. I will not be combative or defensive and I trust what you say at this point.

Phase 1:

Signs of mania, possible hospitalization

- Fast talking
- Big ideas (aka going to a news station to reveal the real reason for autism)
- Not sleeping (2 nights straight)
- Delusions increase (beliefs that aren't based in reality)
- Paranoia increase (like someone is poisoning my food or recording me)
- Taking on too much
- S*icidal thoughts rooted in religious delusions. **Immediately go to hospital** (thinking I'm Jesus and I have to die to save the world)
- Talk about God a lot
- Lack of insight into the impact of symptoms (will deny I have bipolar)
- The world's problems are all mine to take care of.

- Talking about light a lot
- Meditating a lot
- Mentioning water too much
- Mentioning Michael Jackson too much

Phase 2:

What I personally do when in mania

1st Step
- Talk self down
- Slow speech down
- Look in the mirror
- Play slow music
- Body awareness exercise (check in with each body part starting with feet)
- TELL PEOPLE WHAT IS GOING THROUGH MY HEAD

2nd Step
- Call Psychiatrist – Dr. E Phone #
- Call Psychologist – Dr. R. Phone #
- Call Nurse Practitioner Phone #
- Immediately call 1 of 3 main contacts so I'm not alone in the house

Jane Doe 1 (partner in Fort Collins) Phone #
Jane Doe 2 (sister in Berthoud) Phone #
Jane Doe 3 (friend in Johnstown) Phone #

Other people to call

Jane Doe 4 (a friend who will let my San Diego friends know) Phone #
Jane Doe 5 (a friend who will let my Colorado friends know) Phone #

*Get my family involved as soon as **second step** has hit. See if anyone can come to Colorado for immediate support.

Phase 3:

What other people can do
Have me read The Plan. Go over it with me
Reassure me that I'm just Veronica

Say these specific things:
- Veronica, are you reading into what I'm saying? You don't need to. Don't read into anything anyone is saying to you.
- Do you think you have to die to save the world? You aren't supposed to die. People need you here as Veronica.
- Do you think men are controlling women? They aren't. You have thought that every time you become manic.
- *If listening to music: Are you reading into the lyrics? You don't need to.
- **If I'm in the ER** and still out of it (even if my eyes are closed) "Veronica, they are not going to do surgery with no anesthesia on you. No one is going to hurt you in any way."
- Is that the truth? (Useful when I am saying something that sounds not true or delusional)

These six points can be brought up frequently as I tend to go in and out of reality at seemingly spontaneous times and frequencies.

*(If I say I am God/Jesus etc.) You are not Jesus or God. You are Veronica. The world isn't going to end and you don't need to save anyone. Remember you have already been hospitalized for this and that is what you thought then too.

Phase 4:

Hospitalization

****Do not use an ambulance if possible. Find someone to drive me****
(This is because of cost)

Name of hospital:
Address:
Phone # to ER (**Helps to call ahead**)

Back-up hospital:
Address:
Phone #

Last resort hospital:
Address:
Phone #
Current Medications as of 12/2023:

3 mg Vraylar
1 mg Lorazepam (Ativan) as needed (if I'm not sleeping)

Phase 5:

Discharge Planning

Where to stay:
- In my own home with friends and partner taking turns
- With partner or a close friend that feels they can help. JUGGLE ME! Not just one person taking care of me for days on end. House to house is fine.
- In a friend's home that is not close to the coastline
- Last resort with my sisters.

Remember: You are not a burden. People will be there to help.

What to avoid:
- Strangers
- Men (I don't trust them)
- Work
- Ocean/Coastline/Water (I have a recurring delusion that I need to drown myself to save the world)
- Sarcasm and metaphors (I won't understand them)
- Internet
- Music with words (I think the words are about me)
- Any television or movies (I think the actors are speaking to me)
- Children (I think they are the only ones who can always see that I'm God, so I will try to talk to them)

I send "The Plan" to everyone I personally come in contact with. That includes my boss, coworkers, family, friends, and people in need of their own plan. The support system and person with mental illness can have a conversation while the one being supported is lucid. Coming up with a phrase like "We are on the same team" can help when the person may become manic which may look like agitation, confusion, or excitement. Certain phrases have calmed me down in the midst of delusions. Find your own phrases and tricks that may work.

45

Impact of Me

Another year passed, and Lindsay and I broke up. Ultimately, bipolar wasn't the final blow to our relationship but it shaped us both in ways we didn't expect. Lindsay and I both started writing, recording, and performing songs about bipolar I. We both realized how important it was to write music together and so we had to step away from our intimate relationship. Looking through my lens as the one affected directly and looking through her lens as the caretaker, we educated on the matter through song. We always talked about it on stage between songs which eventually led to Lindsay opening up about her panic attacks and high anxiety.

I wondered what it would be like to date someone who had this hibernating thing they'd never seen awake. I felt like I was hiding a very scary monster from Lindsay when we first met. Would it feel like I'd be lying if I didn't go into grand detail about what could happen again? What could put my next partner in a very hot seat that they didn't sign up for? It's one thing to say, "Hey, just so you know, I have bipolar I," and quite another to see it in action.

The impact of my episodes on others in short, was traumatic. Some of my friends still process it with each other. Everyone was so young at the time and none of us were equipped. How could I date or marry someone, knowing they might also be left with these traumas? I need and want support, and I don't ever want to allow one person to take care of it all, the way Noelle and Lindsay took care of me day to day. It's important to also have the Christine's of the world and/or family—friends on the outside of all the intimate relationship things that go on.

I imagine dating me when I'm "off" is in ways like dating someone with severe dementia. I've worked with this population through the years as a music therapist and now as a music performer. I just "go with it" when someone is talking about something that doesn't seem to be based much in reality. Trying to convince someone in this state that they are in fact wrong can cause anxiety, agitations, and confusion for them. In the same way, gently guiding me to a safe space happens easier when everyone plays along.

46

Third Times a Charm

Thursday, January 7, 2016, thirty-three years old, four days until hospitalization

I had gotten rid of over half of my clothes, and it felt really good. I first went through my t-shirt drawer. I had three rows of t-shirts and I had to make sure they were all the same height. I took off my pajama sweatshirt and picked out a shirt to wear. I put it on—it was the picture of a record. I looked down to read the name of the band on the record. The album title, which was also the t-shirt company said, "Supreme Being." I had never noticed this, and I didn't read it until I put it on.

It is a sign. Nothing is by chance. I am in fact THE Supreme Being.

I gave away clothes that I never wore but had deep emotional attachment to. I even threw away underwear I didn't like to wear. I felt clear. I got inside my closet and washed the floor and walls. I was always scared to clean it out because I didn't know what gross, dirty things I could find after two years of neglect.

Everything I did had some type of symbolism connected to it.

I am getting the skeletons out of my closet. I am going into the dark corners of my mind and witnessing the unknown.

I pulled everything out from the drawer below my sink and just started trashing things without a second thought.

I organized my shoes by color. Then I organized my ties by color and pattern. This sounds easy, but when you have sixty-two ties, it takes a while. And yes, I just counted them. I then organized my short-sleeve button-ups by solid color and then by pattern color, then did the same with my long-sleeves. I finished by organizing my jackets in this fashion. The hangers were next. They all had to be a certain shape and made out of wood or plastic. There was so much chaos inside, a feeling of being overwhelmed and on overload had come over me. I had to find a sense of normalcy and control.

A quick ramp-up to mania, and on January 11, 2016, I was hospitalized for my third manic episode.

I reopened my laptop and started writing this chapter after only being out of the hospital for a month.

In my head: right medications + right team + right support + fall/winter season = no breaks. My belief that I would be manic-free in the winter months and that I would only have to be on alert in the warm sunny seasons was disproven. My idea that if I checked off all the right boxes, I would win, was incorrect. I do not think I can outsmart myself. I now have the gratitude in my heart to cherish the times in between breaks. I made it over four years with no mania. Up to this point, it was my longest stint.

This break was different in a lot of ways. I felt grounded through the bulk of it. My peak hypermania lasted approximately a day and a half. My big paranoia and big delusions tapered off at a rapid rate—only two days' worth leading up to going to the ER, with some tiny flare-ups that I was able to ward off for four to five days until I was eventually hospitalized after a sleepless night.

Around this time, I took a three-day course on Transcendental Meditation (TM). There were many scientific benefits linked to the practice, and I was looking for a change and wanted to focus on spirituality. I started doing the meditations twice a day, like the instructors guided us to. It was only twenty minutes for each meditation.

I started feeling particularly "up" about a week and a half before this episode. The meditations and increase in mania tendencies coincided. There is no way to really know if it was purely coincidence or not. To play it safe, I stick to walking meditations where my eyes are open and I am aware of what is going on.

My recollection of feeling truly delusional only dates back to January 7. Becca, someone in my life at this point with whom I was in an undefined stage of a new relationship, noticed something I said around January 4.

Becca:
"A week before the break, you were talking about a friend back home who was going through a hard time. She kept coming up in your meditations, and you reached out. Then you used a phrase that stuck out as peculiar to me. You said, "She's safe now."

This was new territory for Becca. I was in my early thirties, and she was ten years younger than me. And while Becca looked young, it felt like she had been on this planet before. Always a thought before she spoke, and it was rare that Becca would react before thinking. And while she was compact in stature, she had a voice. Not just a powerful singing voice, but a voice that would speak up for others.

Becca was a music therapist for the same company I had worked at during my first manic episode. The company that fired me. I came to Becca's workplace to lead a "Guitar Skills Needed for Music Therapists" course. We left the in-service that day, neither of us really thinking much of the other. We later ended up being at the same house concert where I actually had to use a cane because I had stepped on glass, which is where I got the endearing nickname, "Gramps," from Becca. Fast-forward, and we were at the same party with mutual friends and she mentioned being gay, and my eyes lit up. I hadn't seen her yet. I never really assume anyone is gay or straight but I guess looking back, I really didn't think she was gay. Becca, twenty-three, the age that I charted new territory and moved to San Diego, gave me back a sense of freshness and of youth. She taught me that I'm "not old" (even though she called me Gramps). Becca was a powerful artist in her own right, and in my eyes, always seemed ready and willing to do the internal work that every person must eventually do if they want to grow.

I had a very hard time attaching to Becca as a partner. I think there was some shame about our age difference, but I also just had a hard time committing to one person intimately in general. It took a long time before I started referring to her as my partner or showing affection in public. It took me years more to realize all along I was meant to be ethically non-monogamous.

Becca:
"During the start of your climb into mania, I called Christine to talk to her about some of the things you had been doing and saying that seemed unlike you—basically, I wanted to "ring the alarm" so to speak, so the people who needed to could set the wheels in motion. I remember pacing around the house while I was on the phone and trying to get my thoughts in order. I tried to be objective and only give her the clinical information while actively choking down all of my feelings about it, which seemed really difficult at the time."

I was feeling very self-assured that week before the break. My friend, Toby, was having trouble finding a good price on a car. I told her I would send out the car vibes.

"Don't worry. It will happen." I sat down and envisioned the perfect car for a great price. A few days later she had a car, and I *"knew"* a big reason it happened was because of me.

I was starting to believe I had real psychic abilities. I sometimes look back and wonder, "Is some of this real?" About a week before my break, I reached out to my friend whose sister was going through a hard time. My friend texted back and told me, "It's so weird you texted me." She went on to say that day had been the roughest yet. I kept seeing her sister in my meditations, who was in mourning from the loss of a child. Around that time, I also texted a dear friend who had been going through tough stuff. He said I must be in touch because he was having a hard moment when I texted. I would be thinking about someone and then they would text me five minutes later. I'm not sure if when heightened like that I really am picking up on more sensitive information or if that part is in my head. Maybe I'll never be able to answer that question.

47

Not ALL Bad

My first manic episode started as depression. The last two episodes started off in hypomania. This is still mania but not as extreme. A person won't end up in the hospital for hypomania. From my perspective, hypomania makes everything focused and clear.

There are moments in which hypomania has benefits. Having a mental illness itself comes with many benefits. Generally, creativity, compassion, and innovations come exploding from people who have mental illness, many times in the midst of a crisis. The canvas touched by Van Gogh who was touched by bipolar, would have looked different if he had a different brain. One of his most famous paintings, starry night, was done from the window of the asylum he was in. There is a depth to art that comes from intensity. There are many benefits to having bipolar that do not get lost when taking medications if the dose is appropriate.

It's true: Hypomania can be a superpower.

Alex:
"In hypomania my grades started going up."
And truer that hypermania can be detrimental.

Alex:
"In hypermania I started drawing on my essays and writing profanities."

In hypomania, everything makes sense, and life is easy. Part of this ease comes with letting go of most of my fear and worry. However, hypermania smudges the lens of my perception. The sunny days with rose-colored lenses are switched out for darkness and night-vision goggles. To date, I have stopped many episodes from becoming full blown. From the small sample of big explosions, my pattern generally goes something like this:

Step 1.
Hypomania—I'm doing a lot and creating a lot. This is hard to detect because I already create and do a lot. More than anything, creation is an indicator that my brain is active. In the hypo-state I think everyone likes me and everyone wants to be with me. My worries have all melted away and fear goes away, which means risk goes up. I'm so confident and people have noticed and told me. I'm usually aware of the fact I am in a hypomanic state, so there is a hint of caution. Not every hypomania has turned into a full-blown episode for me. I email/text/call my main people to clue them in and stay on alert. I start taking a sleep aid at night if I need to.

Step 2.
Euphoric mania—this is generally short-lived. It also comes and goes. I always think I am God or some part of the trinity. I can also go in and out of thinking I am a current pop culture figure like Michael Jackson. I have the epiphany that my music will *literally* change the entire world. I am trying to convince my friends I'm fine.

Step 3.
Dysphoric mania—This eventually happens, and it is the one I remember most. Probably because it is the most traumatic. People are going to end my life, I have to die to save everyone in the world, or I imagine failing the world and suffering the consequences. I have to go back to hell for 2000 years and try to save everyone again once the 2000 years is up, only to fail again and do it all over. I see the disappointment on my niblings' faces because I didn't do my job. Now, they are all going to suffer. People are starting to realize I am the divine, so they will try to take my divinity. They will do anything to me to get to it.

Step 4.
Rapid cycling—After hours of thinking I have to die again; I realize I actually DID do my job. This is the new life. Heaven will forever be on earth, and we will all be united. I am the King. No. I'm wrong. Everyone is turning on me. I cannot trust anyone. I go back and forth.

Step 5.
Hospital—This is the point where I am on the way to or at the ER. Thus far, every time I've gone into the ER, I have thought *the staff is going to torture me now.* That someone would be performing surgery on me with no anesthesia. *I know there will be a struggle, but in time I will save everyone. It will not be easy, and I will suffer a lot.*

Step 6.
Lights out—I'm handcuffed, restrained, or strapped down as staff inject me with something to knock me out. This has happened at all three hospitalizations because I have "lashed out" to protect myself in that environment every time. I have always lashed out at this point due to some type of delusion, paranoia or hallucination.

Step 7.
Recovery time—I generally go into a moderate or severe depression after coming back to reality, and I think that is a human thing and not a bipolar thing. Anyone would feel low after going through so much.

Thanks to technology, in this third episode, I was able to look back through the calendar on my phone as a research point for this book. My schedule got heavier as the days moved on.

At this time of purging many of my belongings, I reached out to some mutual friends I shared with Becca (like Toby) because I was getting rid of a suitcase. One of them wanted my suitcase, so I drove over to drop it off. Toby was there and we sat on the couch and talked.

Toby:
"You said you knew *'something big was coming.'* You said you were scared because you knew it was going to be big, but you felt calm because you knew you could handle it. You said it was big, but it was different."

Toby noted that I had brought this thought up until the night before the break of my manic episode. She reviewed The Plan.

Toby:
"I just couldn't tell the difference between a lack of insight, which is one of your symptoms in "The Plan" or was it insight because you said it was different. And it was different. From previous episodes, it sounded and looked like you were acting and handling it differently.

"I kept wondering, 'Is she right about that?' You were talking a lot about people from home and stuff from growing up. When you left, you texted, 'You've always been grounding for me. Thank you for listening and laughing. It helped.' From then into the last day, I was hanging with you (January 10), you got so normal and 'yourself' when you were cracking up laughing."

Later that night, I had a solo show at a coffee shop in San Diego. I practiced for a big portion of the day leading up to the show. Performing always leaves me feeling a bit "up." Nothing out of the ordinary for that scenario. I went to bed a bit later than usual but slept eight hours.

Friday, January 8th

I canceled a guitar lesson because I knew something wasn't right. Then, I went to Lindsay's house for band practice and kept telling her she was being negative. I wanted to change some of her lyrics because they were, "too negative." I know she was concerned about me, but I told her not to worry because worry affects me in a negative way. We went to a restaurant, and I was already pretty gone. I just wanted Lindsay to send me love. On the way back from a restaurant, I started to believe I was seeing signs in people. People that in my mind at the time, were awakened. A tall and slender black man with big dreads and flowy pants that one may associate with meditation and spirituality was walking past us at the crosswalk and we looked at one another.

We recognize each other on a divine level. I was seeing signs in everything in the environment and felt like I knew my future. *I can see it.* I was very self-assured. The sweetness of the edge of hypomania.

Later that day, I went to my appointment with my friend and Reiki Master Dr. L, for Reiki. In short, Reiki is an energy healing and clearing. About a week before I was mentioning to her that I was feeling detached and not very grounded. I had a lot of energy building inside me.

Alex also seeks counsel from holistic healers during the ascent into mania. He was able to predict one out of five of his manic episode escalations.

"I was doing spiritual work on myself. I was trying to get energy to run through my body. I was working with someone. I was doing movements to get it to move. I had a blockage in my solar plexus, it felt filled like putty. I worked on opening it up, and as soon as I felt it, I think something happened energetically, and it tried to reestablish itself. I felt it coming on. As soon as something got cleared, I thought, 'Shit. I'm getting manic.'"

The other four out of five times looked different.

Alex:
"It's kind of like a Dr. Jekyll, Mr. Hyde thing. Or you just don't notice the transitions because when you're hypomanic, you feel good, and when you're manic, it's too late. You're Mr. Hyde."

The Reiki session lasted about an hour and a half. By the end, I felt like I was channeling Jesus, and we processed that together. I was toying with the idea that I might be Jesus. Dr. L noted that Jesus is a great healer. That helped me to stay in my body. In that moment I was able to maintain that "I am Veronica, and Jesus is Jesus."

That night I called Christine and Molly, and we all went to Toby's house. Becca was unavailable. I needed to be around people that "knew" about this. People I felt comforted by. There were four other people in the room.

I felt like Christine and Molly were having such a loud conversation. It felt like they were talking so fast. People were talking over other people. I couldn't make sense of what everyone was saying. I could hear the movements in the house, I could see arms acting out conversations in gestures and people's faces changing and contorting as they laughed what I perceived as a deafening laugh. A common symptom of mania bubbled: difficulty processing my external environment and going into sensory overload. Everything looked and sounded chaotic.

Emotions were building, and I grabbed Toby's guitar and just started finger picking. The chatter got louder and louder. They were talking about the movie, "Room." They were describing a scene in which a man kidnaps a woman and abuses her every night. I asked them to "Please be quiet" and "Don't talk about that." I saw it as negative. I couldn't see the point in talking about negative things. It got quiet and then the chattering was at a low roar. The chattering multiplied, and I put my head on the guitar and started crying silently. I started shaking and more firmly, I asked them to stop. I stood up and the sobbing bouts started, so I put my arm over my mouth to silence what was to come. Part of me didn't want Toby and other newbies to see me like this. I didn't want it to scare them. I was existing in a few worlds at the same time.

I walked into the backyard. Molly and Christine followed. Christine told Toby and the others to stay inside because there were too many people. I started bellowing and sobbing. Molly and Christine were holding me and consoling me. "Breathe, V." Streams of tears came out. I would become silent and calm until another wave of anguish came over me. I was shaking so hard. My whole body convulses significantly when I cry like that. I cannot control the shaking, and I need other people to be near me when it escalates. It is difficult to console myself in this moment. "Breeeathe, V." I hung my head in exhaustion. Quick breaths. A heavy sigh. They helped me up, and we went back to my house.

On the way back, Christine said, "'The Plan is in effect." I kept trying to tell her this was different. I was grounded. And the thing is, I really was. They walked me to my porch, and Christine reiterated "The Plan" and said, "I'm not leaving." Molly looked at me and said, "I believe you, V." After about five to ten minutes of me reassuring them, they left.

I needed someone to empower me, and I needed someone to give me a reality check. Had it gone differently, things could have gone wrong. If they both thought I was fine, Christine wouldn't have been on alert. This was the beginning of a crisis. If they both told me they weren't going to leave, I could have escalated and gotten physical in order to protect myself.

They eventually left, and I called Becca and asked her to stay with me.

Becca noted:

"You were upset on Friday and asked me to come over. I think you knew you were feeling off, which is why you asked me to come over. You were upset about the movie your friends were discussing. You said you needed to be around people, but it was too much energy."

Friday came to a close. I got a good night's rest.

48

Sage Advice

Saturday, January 9th

I went to Little Italy, this charming neighborhood in San Diego, to meet up with my friend. I was having a hard time finding parking but didn't feel frustrated in the least. *The spot I was going to find was going to be just the spot for me.* The spot was very far from my destination. I got out and took it as an opportunity to exercise and people and scenery watch. The meeting was brief, and I headed back in the direction of my car. I ran into a farmer's market and walked through the swarms of people. It felt as if I was in a sturdy boat inching along a glassy sea. Nothing and no one would be getting to me today. I was strong. I got in my car and drove to Subterranean Coffee to talk with my friend, who knew a lot about nutrition. I was making changes in my life. I wanted to change my eating habits. I hadn't eaten too much that day because I felt a bit nauseous and was not interested in eating. I ordered a salad as we chatted. I looked up, and who was ordering coffee? Mr. Big-dreads-flowy-spiritual-pants himself. The man I passed on the street the day prior.

The time is coming. People are starting to recognize I have a divine presence.

I then went to my psychiatrist appointment with Dr. E. that I already had it in the books. I told him about transcendental meditation. During our meeting I shared my experience with Dr. L and told him about empaths. I made reference to Jesus and Michael Jackson. I said it seemed like they were also empaths. He had never seen the escalation into a manic episode. He didn't realize these two people were such hot topics during mania which, in retrospect, sort of blows my mind. I don't know how after all that time, we never touched on those two characters as being warning signs. I told him I felt like the meditations were heightening my awareness. After I was discharged from the hospital, he told me our discussion on January 9th didn't alarm him. Everything I was saying made sense. I was present and grounded. He could see how a person who regularly meditated might have such thoughts.

I got in my car and drove to yoga. The light spilled into the windows and my brow was furrowed as I searched the check-in room where they sold mats and other yoga-type items. I asked, "Do you have any sage?" Sage is known for clearing bad energy and I couldn't get rid of the bad feeling. "We have sage spray but none to burn." I bought it hoping it would have the same effect. I walked back to my car, I placed my finger on the spray bottle, and pushed and pushed and pushed. My face was wet from the mist of the sage and the beginnings of tears. I inhaled slowly and deeply and let out a long sigh.

Once home, I started spraying my living room, kitchen, and all corners of my home. I went up to the bedroom and did the same. As the bottle emptied, my thoughts filled up the space. It was still light out, so I felt safe. I could tell that my mind was starting to give out on me, like my thoughts weren't really coming from me.

My friend had a book launch party that I was supposed to go to. I felt iffy but pushed myself to be out of the house.

I was in a different world but not so different that everyone could notice. A friend seemed to be checking in with me throughout the event. I remember thinking that she did, in fact, sense something was off at that moment, but I was pretty elevated, slightly confused, and somewhat self-assured. There was a distant thought from what seemed like another lifetime that whispered, "You might want to be alarmed."

Friend at the book launch:
"You weren't high energy. It was almost like you were holding yourself together. It's like you didn't appear to be in pieces because you were working so hard not to be. I looked over, and you were holding a glass, and it was shaking a little bit. You weren't saying anything, and you weren't holding anyone's gaze. Before you could connect eyes and smile, you would move on to someone else. You were never focused on anything. You were listening to the music, and it looked like you were emotional like it was affecting you. When I walked over to you, I said, 'Do you want to be held right now?' and you said, 'Yes.' I put my arms around you, and you really held on. You give very intense hugs usually, but this was different. It was like you were really holding on."

The book launch was close enough to the coastline that you could see the ocean. I was paying attention to the live music being played, and I could feel tears accumulating. At one point, a woman whom I had never met was standing next to me. She started sniffling and from the corner of my eye, I could tell she was moved and emotional, too. I put my hand on her back. After about thirty seconds, she reciprocated and put her arm around me. We swayed back and forth to the music. I found myself in one-to-one conversations with strangers, and I wanted to know everything about them. She was the only one I really talked to the whole night, but it was very intense in my mind. I could only focus on one thing at a time.

Becca:
"You texted me that you were coming to a book launch party that I was going to be at. I got to the book launch and was saying hello to everyone. You said hello and kissed me. We left together and had dinner. Everything seemed pretty normal. We got back to your place and played the piano. Everything was fine. I brought up the fact that you kissed me in public at the book launch. You said you just weren't afraid anymore. We had just had conversations about not doing that in public, and I just thought it was very abrupt. Saturday night, you were looking at me and tearing up. You were leaning on me, and it was good that you were."

After the launch, Becca and I went out to eat. We went to dinner near the coast, and I wanted to go to the ocean. This sounds like a completely innocent thing, but in retrospect, it was for manic reasons. I'm not sure if Becca had done a full review of "The Plan" and I was past the point of suggesting going over it together.

I remember feeling nauseous, and I felt like I was on overdrive. The only difference was how rooted I was still feeling. Had I not felt grounded, I would have probably told Becca, "I may have to go to the hospital soon."

I ordered a very healthy dinner with a carrot juice that night with Becca because part of me knew I had to do anything and everything I could to stay "here." I choked down as much dinner as I could because I had been neglecting my food intake for a few days. I generally eat less when I'm feeling up. It's my high-energy response as well as my response when I'm feeling nauseous (generally a side effect of meds). And for me, if I'm becoming manic, less food equals more mania. I told Becca I needed to stay away from someone in my life who had a lot of negative energy and while this might be a very normal thing I usually do, it was strike two. Ocean and energy. If one sign of mania on "The Plan" shows up in a matter of a day it isn't much of an alarm because I do talk about energy and taking people's "stuff" on. But if more than one symptom pops up in a matter of a few hours, something is probably off. I was living in both worlds at this moment because I was aware that I wasn't being myself but I couldn't stop it.

Becca:
"[Saturday night] I still wasn't sure if you were okay. I was dog sitting and asked you to come feed the dogs with me. You were defensive and asked me why I wanted you to come. You said it was fine but then asked to be dropped off at your house to do your meditation."

After I did my meditation, I asked Becca to come back and stay the night.

Becca:
"That night, you went out to your balcony and came back in to lie on your bed and said, 'I just feel like I need to go to the ocean.' I told you it was too cold, and we should wait, which seemed to get your mind off of it."

Sunday, January 10

I ended up waking around 5:00 or 6:00 a.m. and this is not typical for me. I woke up, got up, and started cleaning my bedroom. I remember feeling like I didn't have the ability to figure out the most efficient way to clean. Becca shared her perspective on this morning.

Becca:
"The morning of Sunday you woke up at 5:00 a.m. At 6:00, you asked if you could clean the house. It was loud but also very unorganized. You were moving loud. You aren't usually like that. You would not make eye contact with me all morning. You brought us cereal, and you put down my bowl and said, 'I know I'm not acting like I usually do.' I said that I trusted you, and you were a responsible person. I wasn't worried."

49

Water You Thinking About

I went alone to the Universal Unitarian church at 9:00 a.m. While church alone isn't an alarm, church, energy, and ocean are. I hadn't been to this church for a while. It's not an every-week practice.

The other people here can tell I am Jesus by looking in my eyes. Not all of them, just a select few.

I was looking for something (I can't remember what) in a drawer at my house. When I moved things around, I found a rosary I hadn't seen in a while. *This is a sign.* I put it in my pocket. Before church, I was sitting on a bench outside praying the rosary. I looked up, and I saw an old man holding a bag of oranges in a grocery bag. When I went into the church, I saw him again. *This is a sign, I need to sit next to him.* When I sat next to him, we talked momentarily. Two people sat on the other side of me. One of them was his daughter and the other was her husband, so I introduced myself. Their names were Patty and Jorge. When I was younger, I knew a woman named Patty. Patty was our teen life leader's mom. Patty and I became close and would pray the rosary together, and she gave me a big crucifix necklace that I proudly displayed around my neck at all times. I also knew a man named Jorge and Jorge and Patty knew each other very well. They are extremely devout Catholics. Jorge is a visionary and claims to get messages from God, the Virgin Mary, and other religious figures that have passed. He travels the world doing this, and any time he came to town, he would come to our church. He would sing "Ave Maria" at mass, and my mom would accompany him on piano.

Patty and Jorge are visiting through other bodies to assure me I will be safe.

Church started.

The pastor is looking at me.

From where I sat, her eyes were a dark brown. They almost seemed to pop out of her face. *I can see she recognizes the divinity in me. She is smiling at me. Her eyes light up every time she looks over at me.* Part of her sermon was about water, and we sang a song about a river at the end.

The water is a sign I am on the right track. I am on the hunt for The Ultimate Source.

Before church ended, I had to go to the bathroom. Real bad. I didn't want the pastor to see me leave, but to know me is to know my bladder. It's terribly weak, and I'm not above peeing my pants by accident. I somehow kept it all together, so to speak. *If I leave, she will think I am abandoning her* so I waited until the end.

I walked to the bathroom in the church hall, and I heard a woman's voice in a stall about four stalls from me. I looked under the stalls and saw tiny feet dangling from the toilet, and the woman's feet were pointed toward her. I thought, *she is molesting her.* I stayed in the bathroom by the sink to wait for them. The little girl looked at me, and I swear I could see it on her face. I could see the shame of being caught in the woman's eyes, though I'm sure this just wasn't really the case in that moment.

When I am lucid, molestation is something that I might be projecting at times. I can tell when a woman is uncomfortable with a certain man or that a kiddo doesn't feel comfortable around that certain adult. But when I'm manic, it is 100 percent fact in my head. Many times, in mania, I have approached the "abuser" or tried to catch the eye of the "victim" to see if they are, in fact, alright.

Energy + ocean + church + water + sexual assault. These were all red flags in my plan. The moments of madness were adding up.

I left after they left because I didn't want anything else to happen to the little girl. I started walking to my car then abruptly stopped walking and just stood there.

I can't just leave.

I went back into the common area where people meet after church. The little girl was sitting alone, and to me, it appeared like she was about to cry. Her lip was quivering, and when we made eye contact, her face got serious. I sat two seats away from her and the woman she was with sat down.

I looked at the little girl and said, "Are you okay?"

She didn't say anything but nodded once. The woman then introduced herself to me.

She stuck her hand out to shake mine, and I just looked at her. She told me she was this little girl's grandma. The little girl lived in Sweden and was visiting.

I asked the little girl how many days she had left before returning home, and she said, "Five days," and put five fingers up in the air.

Her grandma said, "She is counting the days."

I said, "You're almost there," and left.

I wonder what that woman thought of me.

Had I not waited to go to the bathroom, I wouldn't have seen this incident and reassured the little girl that she would make it. I gave her hope. Hope for a light at the end of this tunnel and hope that Jesus/God is back, alive, and well. The children have been waiting for me to come back.

Two to three days leading up to an episode is when I start to believe I can see which children have endured something hard, and in that state, all children recognize my divinity. I look around at a parent putting a pacifier in their baby's mouth when they cry. In my delusional mind, I see this baby as being oppressed and silenced. *They are trying to tell me something, and the parents don't want me to hear it. They don't want to hear it either.*

But, who wants to hear a crying baby?

As I left church that day, emotions were building. My hand was in my right pocket, where I was white-knuckling my rosary. I started thinking about all the kids who don't have a voice. I started thinking there were kids around the world being abused. I started thinking of the girl at church who was going to be with her grandmother for five more days.

I started driving, and with each passing second, came a new level of sorrow. I called a close friend from back home who is a mega Jesus lover, and I needed someone in touch with him. To be clear, if a person were to ask me if I believe in Jesus currently, I might first say, "It's hard to believe in someone that you think you are sometimes." I see Jesus as a powerful, kind, influential, charismatic person in history and, in some ways, have wondered if he ever struggled with delusions of grandeur. Hot take, I know, but this book isn't meant to change your mind if you are Christian.

Wells of turbulent sorrow were coming from my body. I pulled my car over and cried. I urgently asked my Jesus-believing friend to pray for me. I told her everything that happened. She prayed Jesus would give me peace. She told me, "Jesus loves you so much, Veronica." That sentence brought me back into my own skin because she referred to two people. I was back to being Veronica for the moment.

When I'm in mania, a seemingly insignificant statement can change my perception and bring me back to the world. It can also create an alternate world.

I put my car in drive and headed to Toby's house. Toby and Becca were there.

Becca:
"You came in and sat down. You were going back and forth between sobbing and laughing and joking. You were sobbing so hard you couldn't hold your cup. You didn't say why you were crying."

Toby:
"When you came over for breakfast, you were visibly shaking and trying to catch your breath. I made you tea. We had bread and avocado. It looked like you were trying to force yourself to eat. You talked about the little girl you saw at church. You told us that the little girl would be going back to Sweden and said, 'She'll be safe there.' Becca and I looked at each other. You talked about the pastor talking about water. and it was raining that morning. and you said you didn't know what it meant. We just started talking about something else. and you were laughing. and you were totally yourself again. Normal breathing. You were calm. When you went back into thinking about whatever it was you were thinking about, you started to get shaky. All I wanted to do was keep cracking jokes, but I didn't want to be insensitive. Then you said you needed to go to the farmer's market and clean your house."

I had been hyper-focused on getting my hands on some sage to burn, and I knew the farmer's market had some. I wanted to sage my house. I could feel the energy everywhere and needed a clear space somewhere on the planet. On the way to the farmer's market, I decided to just go home. I knew it would be too much for me as many people go to this farmer's market. Even though I was in delusions, I still had the ability to recognize possible triggers. I was still trying to protect myself. To be split in two like this feels like a bizarro world. It's like there is a lucid world, a manic world, and then this third type of world that is ever-changing and hard to put my finger on a way of describing it.

When I got home, there appeared to be chaos in a communal foyer of my house. It's a big two-story yellow house that is split in thirds. My front neighbor's washer (which was close to my door) flooded, and there was water everywhere. *Another sign.* Michael (neighbor) was the one working on it. *I don't trust him.* I pulled a piano book out of a shelf that I hadn't seen in a while. It was Rich Mullins: a Christian artist. It really brought me back to my religious times as a teen. The front cover is a picture of him covering his face.

He is covering his face because he can't see the truth in my eyes. Men are trying to control things, and they know if they look into my eyes, they won't be able to handle it.

After a while, I just started improvising on the piano and eventually played "Let There Be Peace on Earth." Peace was heavy on my mind. *Jesus brings peace and I bring peace. There must be peace on earth soon. My final hour is coming.* My feelings started becoming too much. I decided to call Christine. She came over, and we sat on my bed and talked. During our conversation, she told me they sang "Let There Be Peace on Earth" at her church that day. *Another sign.*

Christine:
"We talked a lot about religion. We had both just gone to church, and you talked about the girl who "was" molested at your service. You told me something big was coming, and you were just trying to listen to that. You talked about how people feel like they have to put people in psych wards that have special abilities. I asked you if the thoughts had anything to do with bipolar and you said, 'No. This is different.' We talked about "Star Wars." We talked about how the new villain is a bad guy,

but he has a little light in him that is pulling him, which is the opposite.

"I was probably at your house for two to three hours. You thanked me for coming. You said right before I knocked, you were sitting on your bed and holding on to your rosary. You joked about the Cup of Truth because you had been drinking a lot of water."

A few hours after Christine left, the Cup of Truth delusion manifested.

Christine:
"When I left, it felt okay to leave you alone. It didn't feel like you were going to hurt yourself. Your demeanor was calm, but the things you were saying were off. You were saying you were channeling Jesus, and that none of this had to do with bipolar."

I still wasn't in a good place, so I called Toby. She was doing paperwork but said she could come to my house to do paperwork. When she got there, I felt like a busy bee. I started going through my clothes and belongings again to get rid of more stuff. I didn't know what to do. I was standing up and sitting down, playing the piano, and lying on my bed.

Toby:
"You were just cleaning your room. You were putting stuff in a giveaway pile. You said you needed to get rid of your charcoal pencils and pastels. I asked if you used them and you said you did."

I was in the kitchen when my neighbor, Michael, walked in my house. I was letting him use my washer and dryer. He said, "I heard you playing the piano. Were you singing "Peace is Flowing Like a River?" I told him I was. "I have a beautiful version of that song."

Michael decided to put a bunch of songs on a USB and give it to me. I gave him my USB to use. As he left something did not feel quite right about the interaction.

> *He is trying to assert himself by walking into my house and using my washer and dryer. He wanted me to have all of these songs that are about men and empowering men. There may even be a virus on my USB and he could have stolen things off of my USB. I should have given him a blank one.*

Paranoia. Delusions.
At one point I was upstairs with Toby and told her I was going downstairs to get an orange. She told me she had oranges with her, and it made me think of the old man with oranges at church. *This is a sign. I can trust Toby.* From that point on in my break, I wanted Toby around because of this.

Toby:
"After that, you were pretty good that afternoon and evening. Then you lied down for a while, and you were calmly breathing and fell asleep for a while. Everything went downhill when V (a neighbor) and Eloise (V's baby) arrived."

V brought two or three children's books with her. I was reading into everything her baby, Eloise, was doing. One of the books they brought was, "Down by the Bay."

Toby:
"When she brought that book I thought, 'Is this a joke?' She had no idea. It was so strange to me because you kept pointing out things you were reading into, and I could see them. I thought, 'What are the chances that she would bring this book right now?' I was in a state of clear and present mind. I was weirded out and thinking how wild it must have been for you. If I thought it was weird, how scary was it for you? You were fine at first, you were reading a zoo book. But when you read the book about water, you stopped halfway through. Eloise was walking around and trying to play with a broom. You kept saying, 'I know she is trying to say something. Babies know so much. She is trying to talk, and I just want to know what she's

saying.' V asked if you were okay and got to the point that she needed to leave."

After my break I told Michael if I ever appear to be hypermanic, he and Eloise should not come and see me. Written in my plan: I do not trust men, and I think children have the answers. This is why I would approach a child I don't even know sometimes. A parent could take it the wrong way.

Becca showed up unexpectedly, and after a while, I asked her to leave. *I cannot trust her.* Months before this break, she bought me a necklace with wheat dangling on it. I had talked about how much I missed Colorado and home so the wheat was a reminder of growing up on the farm. I loved that piece of jewelry.

She knows I miss home and the farm. I don't ever take this necklace off. She's trying to control me with it. How could I be so stupid and not see this?

Toby was about to leave my house.

Toby:
"In my mind, I thought maybe you were okay. I don't know whether it was insight or lack of insight. I asked if you were good, and you said yes...

"I said, 'Do you want me to stay?', and you said, 'Yeah, maybe you should stay.' We talked for a long time, and we started talking about "Star Wars." I was trying to act normal around you. You kept saying it was frustrating for you that someone contacted your sister [about my recent behavior] without telling you. You were annoyed when someone came over without announcing. You said you didn't want people to freak out because that made you feel worse. I was trying to keep my cool and act normal. I felt like you would know if I was super guarded. I was trying to talk like I normally would. I knew the things to avoid, but I don't know if I was totally mentally prepared to skirt around them.

"You told me you didn't want to listen to music with lyrics. You didn't want to watch a movie. You knew what was going to set you off. Then you were talking about the divine. You had that Supreme Being shirt on. Everything you said I thought was a weird coincidence. You kept saying we have the divine in us. It was language you had used before when talking about yoga and meditation. It was normal, normal, normal, except for one phrase. It was about having the divine being within you.

"I called Lindsay later that night and told her you were talking about the divine. Lindsay asked if I had wanted to let the divine out, but you hadn't. We went back upstairs. I opened up my computer, and I was showing you a picture. Just trying to distract you but not show you something weird. Then you told me you heard an owl the other day."

50

Hoo Ordered the Owl?

A few days before this I had heard an owl outside my house. I texted my spiritually-in- touch friend, Angela, to ask what an owl represented. She has a book called, "Animal Spirit Guides: An Easy-to-Use Handbook for Identifying and Understanding Your Power Animals and Animal Spirit Helpers."

She didn't text me back the explanation until the next night, which happened to be Sunday night. Toby was with me at the time.

Ding—I got a text message. It was a picture of the owl explanation from the book. Toby describes the moment leading up to me reading the text message.

"Your eyes were closed. Totally calm. You were texting your mom, and I wanted you to fall asleep so I could call Christine to strategize the evening. You reached over to check your phone again, and you sat up and said, 'You know, I'm good. Why don't you go ahead and leave?'"

The reason I reacted this way was because of a text I got from Angela who was responding to my questions about the owl. Angela didn't have a copy of "The Plan" and did not know

I was becoming manic at the time. If she had access to this information, I don't think she would have sent the text.

The text of owl interpretations said: "Meditate in silence and in darkness for a few minutes each evening for the next few days and see what is revealed to you. Be alert to any deception on the part of others, whether they're aware of it or not, and look closely behind any guise that they might wear."

I need to get Toby out of the house because she is trying to stop me from meditating. Toby was tricking me into eating forbidden fruit (the oranges). *I failed the test because I ended up eating the orange she gave me. She cannot be trusted.*

"Toby, you need to go."

Toby:
"You were so insistent and at one point you asked me several times to leave and I said, 'V, I'm just gonna stay. I'm just gonna stay downstairs. I won't make a noise.' You opened the door and said, 'Please leave.' I knew you weren't saying this to me. I knew there was something else you wanted to do or some space you wanted. I didn't want to push it and have something happen.

"I only left because I told Lindsay everything. I had a mix of 'What could happen,' and 'If something happens it is all my fault and I should have stayed.'"

Toby was doing everything in her power to not go. She would change the subject or try to convince me otherwise. She left the house and then called saying she forgot something. I didn't let her come back in. In her eyes, she was trying to stay to protect me. In my eyes, she was trying to impede the process.

When she left, I shut off my lights, locked the door, and closed my eyes to meditate. I continued reading the string of texts that detailed what an owl represented:

"This is a particularly ripe period to tap into the fount of intuitive wisdom that is available to you."

I have opened up the channel through my daily meditations. I am all knowing. The time is now to access everything I can. When I close my eyes, I see the color purple.

The purple moves much like a screensaver on a computer screen. I see purple most of the time during meditations. When I'm manic, it increases. I cannot explain why this happens to me.

Alex B. also sees purple in mania and meditations with his eyes opened or closed.

The next text rolled in:
"Now is a particularly significant time for prophecy, and you will see, hear, or feel events before they actually happen."

Something tells me I am going to suffer. I will be hallucinating in sight and in sound, and physical pain will be inflicted on me. The hour is nearing. The world is about to end unless I can save it. I have to stay focused. I have to stay awake tonight.

And the final text that in retrospect I am glad happened.

"Your most creative cycle now is the night, so set aside time in the evening to work on any projects."

I need to write in my book. This is the creative project.

51

Imposter Jesus

Sunday night.
    I decided to pee in my bed because I needed to "let everything go."

Alex B:
"I've also peed my pants several times. I think part of it is letting go, and I thought it was cooling down my system."
    The phrase "letting go" comes up a lot when I am at the height of mania. Eventually, the ultimate letting go leads to ending my life, which I do not consider s*icide. I have a friend with bipolar II who in the midst of delusions tried to end things as a sacrifice to the world. I know I wrote about it earlier, but what might look like a selfish act to a loved one, a caregiver, a family member, may in fact be a selfless act in the mind of the person who dies by their own hand.
    I sat on my bed and cracked open my laptop. If there are any grammatical errors or seemingly cryptic statements I will not correct or explain them. I didn't change anything. I just started typing. This is what came out. The actual events I

detailed were true but the beliefs around them were not. I think the wildest twist in all of this is that I actually do know Jason Mraz now and we have recorded two songs and a music video together. At this time though, I did not know Jason Mraz.

Remember the first manic episode when I told Christine I was supposed to have a show with Jason Mraz? Fast forward and my band, The Lovebirds, has a show opening for Raining Jane. Jason is friends with the girls from Raining Jane. They are awesome women. I don't remember much about him at that time but we didn't cross paths at the show. Fast forward years ahead and I am in Jason Mraz' kitchen. I know his roommate and she had Lindsay and I over. I didn't realize it was his house. I was looking around and saw a picture of Jason Mraz looking a lot like Jesus. We laughed about it at the time. He thinks he is Jesus. But he is not.

I am.

He has tapped into the same source that I have. He has seen the other dimension. Do not be fooled. It is all a guise. He has been trying to get in contact with me for a while. For some reason our paths just haven't crossed yet. Jason got his start at Java Joe's. Java Joe's is the only place I've been playing these days. There is something about it. Jason shows up randomly when he isn't on tour. He was supposed to show up on a night I was playing and couldn't make it last minute. Fast-forward and my friend Kim asks me to help out writing a song for Girls Rock Camp San Diego. I get to the building where all the women are and take the reins on the song. There was a videographer there. I hadn't thought much of her then. Fast-forward and we have a second meeting to finish up the rock camp song. The videographer is there and this time we connect. She then shows me a video that she had done. Jason Mraz is in the video. He is dressed so you can't tell who he is. Wearing sunglasses. Fast-forward and, my producer, Jeff, asked me to go to a show there because he heard Jason would be there. Jeff has known Jason for a long time. They ran in the same circles back in the day. I didn't go. He showed up. Jeff hadn't seen him for twenty years.

Fast forward a few days ago and I'm sitting in the car with my friend, Becca. She pops in a CD. It's Jason Mraz' "Love" album. I resonated with his words in a way that no one else does. I know what he is doing. He is trying to win people over with our most sacred resource: Music.

Fast forward and I'm sitting here at this very moment writing. I look to my left where my vision board is. In the center of it I put a unicorn. Jason painted a big black unicorn on his living room wall that says, "fuck ya."

He knows what I know. The only difference is, he is an imposter. An imposter that has been trying to get to me for a very long time. Music is very powerful and he knows it. Music has the power to change the world and to change the minds of people. His message of love is a way to draw people into him. Music controls the world. Everything is vibration.

I've never liked his music. It does not resonate with me. My friend Molly has always loved his music. She also loves my music and is in my band Veronica May and The To Do List. There is a darkness and a lightness to Molly. She used to try and share his stuff with me and I just never got into it.

This isn't about Jason Mraz the body. This isn't about Veronica May the body. This is about dark vs. light. This is spiritual warfare in the making.

This is some God/devil shit, people.

My friends have been on high alert this past week because I've been showing signs of mania. The only difference is, I'm not scared. I'm taking the wheel. The same themes have been coming back. All but the paranoia and delusions. This is because they are based off of fear. When I told my loyal friend, Christine, about what was going through my head she said we had to stick to "The Plan." A thing that I constructed out of fear. She and Molly were with me at the time. Christine (John) said, "I'm not going to leave you." Molly sees what I have. She is torn between the light and dark. She told me that she trusted me. And I know she does. At the moment, she is conflicted. One theme that has been particularly strong is water. I was at church today and there were several songs about water. I live in a big yellow house that is sectioned into three units. My neighbor said, "The washer flooded." I'm getting closer to finishing my album "Awakened" and El Nino comes to San Diego. The studio gets flooded. We have to record the rest of the album somewhere else. And we will. And it's going to change the world. Mental illness is an illusion. Autism is an illusion. Pain is an illusion. Fear is an illusion.

What is not an illusion? Music. Music reveals all things. People channel God and he writes songs through them. It is evident. The harmonies are beautiful, the message is clear, there is not dissonance. People channel the dark, the fear, and it is evident. Dissonant chords, evil message, angry. So, how can we get people of light and love to unknowingly come over to the dark side? We write songs claiming love. The songs are inviting. "Sing along with me, everyone." We are vibration.

Jason Mraz' garage door has his "Love" logo on it. When you walk down his pathway to his studio, the word "love" in his logo is spelled in the steps. We run to love. We seek refuge in love. In the past three or four days I've been eating a lot of avocado. I stood in my kitchen and stared at the empty avocado skin looking for some answer in it. Jason Mraz' house is in an avocado orchard.

Signs are everywhere and in everything. For many many years I've had opportunities to practice vulnerability. Vulnerability is the opposite of fear.

Vulnerability will set you free. It is the key. It is the light.

The veil is being lifted.

During my second episode, I claimed I was Michael Jackson reincarnated. He had been trying to get through to people. Michael Jackson always wore sunglasses. It kept his soul intact. Other souls couldn't suck out the light. He wore them as a protection. He wore them out of fear. The King of pop. He set the world on fire.

Children are our guides. Children are pure love. We are constantly trying to quiet them. They cry for a reason. Now, when I look in a child's eyes, I know they recognize me. I look back at the songs I've written and they have new meaning. If you go back to my lyrics you will see. All darkness is fear.

Music is the answer. Music comes through people and sometimes those people don't even realize what they have really written. I didn't realize it until just now. I've left breadcrumbs.

Before I wrote all of this, I went on Spotify just to listen to Jason Mraz' "Love" album. I wanted to hear his lyrics to find messages of love. Then I saw this picture on his cover photo of Spotify:

His arms outstretched like Christ on the cross. This is the only reason I thought he was imposter Jesus.

It only went from bad to worse from there. I was writing frantically as I thought the clock was ticking to the final second and my heart was pounding. I remember how hard it was for me to organize what I wrote. I kept having to read sentence after sentence, and it was all so broken. I remember wondering, "Why can't I organize this?" It is very hard to organize thoughts in mania, but I wasn't able to come to that conclusion.

It was now pitch black in my house. I didn't know what to do next. I thought of Eloise. *What was V's baby trying to tell me? When she was at my house, she went over to my tiny Casio keyboard and started banging on it. That's it!* I went over to my piano. *I need to sing to save the world!*

I found my Nalgene bottle and filled it up to the top from my water cooler. I chugged it and started to play. *This bottle is the Cup of Truth and my water cooler contains all the truth. No one may touch this.*

I kept wondering what the point of drinking the water was. I felt like it had its place in it all. I closed my eyes and played the piano. My heart would jump if I played the wrong note because I thought the world was in my hands. It was so delicate and I was tired, but there was no way I was going to sleep even if I tried. I would lie on my bed and the urgency of the situation would become too much. I would go back to the piano.

Downstairs for more water and then back upstairs to play the piano.

The wheels started turning and "bingo," I found my delusion.

I read a study on water molecules a while back. There were pictures of different samples of water. Each sample was exposed to different types of music like heavy metal, or classical. They did the same thing with different words being spoken to the molecules like "war," or "bliss." The molecules actually looked healthier when classical music was played and when words like "bliss" were spoken. THAT is why I have to drink this water. I'll play specific notes on the piano and think about positive affirmations while I do it. It will change my entire self on a molecular level. I could even do this at the ocean. I have to drink as much water as I can. I can stand in the ocean and sing the notes that unlock the world into salvation. As I sing in the ocean, all the water in the world will change. The people will be saved for eternity.

I had probably drank a gallon of water or more at this point. Each time I played a note I would think of a positive affirmation.

I am love. I am strength. I am Jesus.

I started getting a little scared. Toby was keeping Lindsay and Christine updated.

Late Sunday, January 10

Christine got to the house so I came downstairs. The first thing she said to me is, "I'm thirsty."

She only came here to access all the truth. She cannot drink this water and she will certainly not drink from the Cup of Truth.

Christine:
"You said, 'Nope, I changed my mind. You gotta go.' I asked if we could just sit for a second and think. You were on the chair, and I was on the couch. You were just in your head. You didn't say anything. You had a worried look. You looked confused like you were trying to figure something out, but you were also flat. Not very expressive. Kind of what you would imagine someone would look like if their wheels were turning. But it wasn't a good thing. You were having difficult thoughts. I closed my eyes to rest and when I opened them you were staring at me. A little creepy. I was just waiting you out."

She is closing her eyes because she is getting messages from the divine. I need to keep my eyes on her so that when she opens them, she will know that I know. There is something about this "Star Wars" movie. Something about how the dark is being pulled toward the light.

I eventually went back upstairs to play the piano.

Christine:
"You gave me a pillow but no blanket. You said I needed to stay downstairs."

As I ascended the steps, I felt like all my senses were on high alert. About three steps up I hear "crinkle."

Christine had brought her empty water bottle and was going to fill it up with water from the water cooler.

I spun around and came into the living room. I was pissed. I wanted to stand in front of my water cooler to protect it.

I remember the thought I had at that moment. *I can't trust anyone.* I felt completely isolated from all the relationships I had developed over the years. *Not even my disciple, John, can be trusted.*

Christine:
"I tried to drink water. You said, 'Nope. Get out.' You were much more forceful this time. 'You gotta go.' I was scared you might hurt me, and you are bigger than me, so I left. I left my keys inside, and you told me not to come back in. You gave them to me, and I left."

I got back to work on writing and creating when she left. This was probably somewhere right around 11:00 Sunday night or midnight on Monday. I was shaking because I was so cold from all the water I had been drinking. I could not close my eyes easily. They were wide, and I felt like I was in a trance.

Christine immediately contacted Lindsay to get someone over to my house.

Lindsay:
"Christine told me that you kicked her out, so I called you. I said, 'Are you okay? Can I come over?' You said, 'I'm fine. I'm really tapping into something right now. I have to go.' I think this was when you were writing. You said, 'I'll call if I need you.' This was around 10:30 p.m. I went home to go to bed and around midnight you called and said, 'Come over. I can't sleep.'"

Christine knew that the water was a possible point of contention, and it was best that Lindsay avoid it—an important point that kept Lindsay in the house for longer once she arrived.

Lindsay:
"You and I spent a good thirty minutes on the phone while you decided whether or not to let me come. It was a really difficult decision for you to make. You sounded quiet and a little scared. I told you that I would just feel a lot better if I could be around you. That way, if you needed anything I would already be there instead of having to come across town. I said I could stay on your couch and do my own thing, and I wouldn't get in your way. Basically, I asked if you would do it for me. You finally

agreed, and we hung up. I was on my way out the door when you called back and said never mind, you didn't want me to come. But I told you I was already on the way, and that I was tired, and could I please come over? I said we don't even have to talk. "You can just leave the door open for me, and I'll be quiet downstairs, and thankfully you agreed to that."

"I had already been by Michael and V's (house neighbor) because you had told Toby to leave and told me I couldn't come over. I just wanted to give your neighbors a heads up that you probably were not going to be coming down and to just be alert."

I kept trying to make cosmic sense of everything. I thought I needed to be alone in this, but there was a part of me that was very scared. Upstairs, I sat facing the wall. The piano at my fingertips. In mission mode, I began to play. Drink water. Play.

Lindsay:
"When I arrived, you were upstairs. I'm sure you heard me come in, but we didn't say anything to each other for a long time. You were playing the piano. Two notes over and over going up the scale and some chanting. I could hear you stop and take long drinks from your water bottle, then resume."

I was shivering hard. For some reason, I was never able to piece together that the water was making me cold.

My piano was against a white wall. I played slow and deliberate as my eyes were glued to the wall as if I were witnessing the unfolding of a universe.

I see the color purple on the wall. It is a rectangular block of purple. I am trying to let my fingers lead but my mind keeps getting in the way. There is a high-pitched ringing in my ears. The pitches are dividing now... like a prism. I am hearing the universal vibrations. I need to find the pitches on the piano. I'm onto something! I'm not sure which note to start on, but I know I have to unlock everything in the world. I just have to figure out which note to start on...I'll take a drink of water.

All the while, my guardian, Lindsay, was back at her post. This time through the eyes of a very dear friend.

If I had opened my eyes any wider, they would have fallen out of their sockets. I kept my stare fixated on the wall as I played.

I know I can't play the wrong notes. It could be life or death. I'm nervous. If I mess up, I have to start over.

Lindsay:
"Eventually, you came downstairs. I can't remember the sequence of all the times you came downstairs. It happened two to three times, but one of the times you came downstairs, you had a super eerie smile. You sat in the chair and stared at me like that from across the room for a while."

When Lindsay and I were together, I wrote a children's book about us called "Hope and Faith." Hope and Faith were the two characters in the book.

Lindsay:
"I asked what you were thinking about, and you said, Hope and Faith. We talked about the story a little bit. You moved to the couch, and you brought up Jason Mraz and said the three of us were supposed to take over the world."

I walked back upstairs. I started thinking of myself as outside of myself at this point. Referring to who I was in the third person. One thing to mention, drowning myself is usually the way that I think I need to end my life to save the world. There have been a handful of times I believed I had to get in a car accident with Molly specifically.

I hear an ambulance outside. Molly and Veronica got in a car wreck and the ambulance is rushing them to the ER. They aren't going to make it. Molly sacrificed her own life so that I will die which will set God free from my body which will save the world.

All the while, I am just sitting at my piano with thoughts on thoughts on thoughts coming through my mind. The blank white wall seemed to have a glow from the moon that was peeking in my bedroom. The white was slowly becoming dark. *This is the darkness slowly taking over. Let it take over. Give in now, Jesus. You might not make it to heaven this time.*

Alex B:
"One time I was in full-blown mania and also kind of sleeping. It felt like I was thrown into hell. It was a painful landscape I was walking through like I was being stabbed. I was able to jump out of it."

One thought that remained persistent was about the "Star Wars" movie. I kept thinking about how the "bad guy" had some light, some good. This was clearly a new delusion. In all episodes, current pop culture references seem to come into my brain. I kept trying to "crack the code." My eyes wide and fixated on the white wall.

The light is stealing the dark for the first time. What does it mean?

Generally, I can find elaborate answers to anything when I look hard enough in mania.

That's it! This isn't about me giving into the dark. The light always prevails. The light is stronger. I have to refocus on the wall with a new hope. I see the light expand but it doesn't expand a lot. I have to fight this, but I am so tired.

I could feel the pulse of my heart in my eyes. Straining to keep them open as wide as I could. I was so awake yet very fatigued. No matter how hard I tried to see more light on the wall, the darkness of the night prevailed.

The gradual silencing of the light is inevitable. The last sliver of white remains. The last shackle is around my neck, and all Satan needs to do is clasp it. I need to give into the darkness. It's slowly starting to swallow up everything. I am allowing it to take the light from my eyes. The singing worked. I just didn't know salvation would look like this. I have to give into the dark world.

Right as the whole wall was about to be consumed by the last piece of darkness, I closed my eyes.

This means I have failed again. The world's destruction is still lying in my hands.

I walked downstairs. Halfway down my stairs is a ninety-degree turn.

At the bend I see a rectangular dark spot about four feet tall. It is a portal into something unknown. Something scary. I know I have to walk through.

As I got close to what I thought was the portal, it disappeared, and so I continued walking downstairs.

Lindsay:
"You came back downstairs after about fifteen minutes of more piano and chanting. This time you were scared. It looked as if there was a serious battle going on in your mind. From time to time, your eyes would well up with tears and your chin would quiver. We lay on the couch facing each other. You asked questions like, 'Do I have to die?' I held your hand and did my best to remind you that you were Veronica, and you didn't have to die. That you functioned best in the world as Veronica, and that sometimes your mind plays tricks on you, making you think you're God."

Lindsay and I sang a song I wrote and a song we wrote together.

"I tried to remind you that we've been through this before and that you were safe. You sang and played "There is Hope," and we sang, "Love is All it Takes" together really quietly. We both cried. The whole time you would stop to take enormous drinks of water and fill up your water bottle. I told you if you got really scared, all you had to do was ask me to take you to the hospital, and you'd be completely safe there. I stressed that there was no need to hurt yourself whatsoever."

The secret of all secrets has come to me!

I started thinking about the two-book series I wrote about our relationship. "Hope," the Hula Hoop, and "Faith," the Bipolar Polar Bear. They represented Lindsay and me.

Then I started thinking about the first book and tried to remember how it ended. I know at some point, Faith and Hope drove down to the beach together.

I know the only way the world is going to be saved is if Jason Mraz helps. I failed yet another test. It would have been simple. Had I gone to the coffee shop the night I was invited; I would have been able to tell Jason Mraz what we needed to do. It would have been so simple and so fun, but I ignored the divine signs. Now there is only one way.

"Do you remember how the second book ended?"

Lindsay:
"I don't know, but they were good stories."

Lindsay must have been so tired. I kept asking her if it had to be this way. She broke down in tears. I thought this was because the truth was being revealed to her slowly. That she was going to have to drown with me. She said, "I wish it didn't have to be this way." What she meant was that she wished I didn't have to have another episode. What I heard was, "I wish we didn't have to die."

At around four in the morning, I texted Molly, "It's time." I felt like I needed her to take me to the beach now. I thought we needed to get in a car wreck on the way to the beach. There was no logic anywhere. Earlier that night, I had thought I already heard the ambulance taking Molly and me away from the car wreck.

When I was a teen, my teen life leader at the church told us about the rapture. "The time when Jesus will return." He told us that there would be three days of darkness leading up to the rapture. In these three days, the earth would be crawling with demons and fire. They would take all the souls that were not worthy.

It was dark out, and morning was on its way.
We are waiting for the three days of darkness.
I could almost hear the claws on my front door. Our conversation went something like this:
"Can we go to the ocean?"

Lindsay:
"Let's wait until morning."
"Am I Jesus?"

Lindsay:
"You think that when you get this way. The world is better when you are Veronica. If this is too much, we can go to the hospital."

I went back and forth. Back and forth. A line from a Florence and The Machine song popped into my mind. "It's always darkest before the dawn."
We are going to get through it.
I felt a little relieved. I could just be Veronica. I could let the divine leave and someone else at a later date could try to save the world. I thought Michael Jackson failed, so it wouldn't be so bad if I passed up the opportunity. By going to the hospital, I would be surrendering. I would be safe, but everyone else would still be in limbo.

I remember I felt like I could trust Lindsay.

In general, Lindsay and Christine are tied as the number one person I trust. They also happened to be the two top people I took things out on during this break.

52

Burning Man

Lindsay:
"You were looking worried and tired. I asked if you wanted to go upstairs and lay down for a bit. I knew you wouldn't sleep but thought maybe you would at least be calm for a while, and I could have some pseudo-rest. You told me you had peed in the bed, and we laughed about it because you 'let' me lay on the side without the pee.

"We laid there for maybe thirty to forty-five minutes, and you didn't talk. You went to the piano and played the same two notes repeatedly. Probably for thirty minutes. After more of the two notes on the piano, I finally asked, 'Why just the two notes?' That's when you got kind of angry and glared at me and said, 'You need to leave!' You said it a few times, but I just kind of shrugged it off and said things like, 'V, that's ridiculous. It's nearly four in the morning—I don't want to drive across town this late! I'll just go back downstairs and get out of your way and you can do your thing. Promise, I won't bug you.' I hurried downstairs to avoid you kicking me out. Thankfully, you let it go and went back to what you were doing.

"You mentioned wanting to go on a walk, and I said maybe we should wait until it's light outside. I think you read into that as 'waiting for the light,' but I just let you go with it because it kept you inside for whatever reason. Eventually, I suggested we go back upstairs and try to lay down for a bit."

I went out to the balcony, and there were birds flying across the sky. I immediately thought of the song, "Feeling Good" that Nina Simone made famous.

"It's a new dawn, it's a new day, and I'm feeling good...."

I got a huge grin on my face; my lip quivered. I couldn't catch my breath. My chest was full. This was the new day. The dawn before a new world had passed. I made it. We all made it. Only one thing left to do.

Lindsay:
"I followed behind you because I was grabbing my blanket and pillow. When I got upstairs, you were on the balcony standing in a puddle. It had been raining, so I thought for a split second it was water, but then I realized you were peeing your pants again. We laughed about it again, and I asked if you were born in a barn, then cringed because of the whole Jesus thing. Thankfully, you didn't catch that. I could tell you didn't care about peeing your pants, so I didn't want to make a big deal about it for fear you would kick me out.

"We got back in bed for a while. At this point, it was six or seven in the morning. All the while, I had been texting Christine to see if she/someone could relieve me because I was EXHAUSTED, and my nerves were totally fried at this point. She couldn't find anyone to cover, so she said she'd call into work and come over. I told you she was coming over and asked her to bring us some food. I think around this time, you were texting Molly."

"Molly, I need my glasses." I had left them at her house a few days prior. I wanted the glasses for protection from the outside world. She texted back that she would come by to drop them off. She also said, "Please tell me what I can do." And I just texted back, "Love." I knew somehow, we needed faith, hope, and love. It was symbolic that Molly was the one handing me protection. She was my counterpart and understood me. She was a guardian. *Molly is going to have to take Jason Mraz's spot and be the missing piece of that trinity of values.* She also has a tattoo on her arm that says, "All You Need Is Love" so I made sense of it.

Lindsay:
"I think you were calling/texting with Steph and asking her to come. She was on her way to New York for your dad's surgery, so she was struggling with what to do."

Shortly after, my sister texted asking what I needed. My heart sank.

I failed another test. Molly was a trap, and she didn't even realize it. I was supposed to get love from my sister. A sister's love. Now, my sister is going to die. My dad is with her, and he will have to die too.

I'd never thought I was a cartoon before. I've always been told I was very animated. There's a first time for everything, I guess.

I am Ana and my sister is Elsa [from the animated movie *"Frozen"*]. This delusion did not last long, but I know I had it because it was in current pop culture, and my sister texted asking what I needed. I said, "Love." SPOILER ALERT— Anna saves Elsa at the end of the movie. It was a sister's love that prevailed.

Since I told Molly I needed Love, she took it and now my sister cannot.

I then started to believe I was "piecing things together." *The main song in the movie is called, "Let It Go."* I was replaying the melody of the chorus. "Let it gooooooo. Let it gooooooo" and then I started to "piece together" more nonsense. *Let it go! Let go of everything! Even my pee! THIS is why I have to keep peeing my pants! I am Ana! My sister has been sending me hidden messages in her songs!* I smiled an all-knowing smile every time I peed. And oh boy, did I pee. At this point I had easily downed over a gallon of water and it. Needed. Out. The combination of the Cup of Truth and "Letting Go" made for very clear pee. I was out of it, and dangerously hydrated.

Lindsay:
"When it finally approached daytime, I started gently suggesting that you let me call the psychiatrist. I said things like, 'He knows you; he cares about you, he's helped you before, and maybe, he'll have some suggestions for ways we can help quiet your mind a little bit.' After a lot of this, you finally agreed to let me call.

"As soon as I started calling though, you were very nervous about it and started to get agitated. I left him a message. He called back about ten minutes later when you were either on the phone or going downstairs to get your glasses. I can't remember how, but you were distracted, which allowed me to talk to him about what was going on and get a quick appointment scheduled for 1:00 p.m."

Remember, I do not usually trust men in this state.

Lindsay is calling my male psychiatrist. He is controlling her. All the men are controlling Lindsay. And my mom. And my sister. And all the women in the world. I have to get rid of all the men in this house.

I have to act fast. Time is ticking and Lindsay is being controlled over the phone. He knows the fate of all mankind is in my hands.

Lindsay:
"I walked outside where you were and said something like, 'Good news, he can see you at 1:00 p.m.' But from that point on, you weren't having it. You said, 'Nah. I don't need to go.' You looked pissed, almost like in a cocky way. You walked back

inside and started grabbing pictures off your fridge and walls in a frenzy. I asked what you were doing."

I know exactly what to do in order to free everyone. I have to go inside the house and go into my hallway where the family photos are hung.

Lindsay:
"You basically ignored me. You were on a mission. I was more concerned with the glass in the frames until I saw you start to look for a lighter."

I will look into the eyes of all the men in each photo. If I see evil in their eyes, I will burn the photo. It will set the women in my family free. I will set the women of the world free.

Only one man was left unburned in the whole ordeal. Mark (brother-in-law), you are the sole male survivor.

Lindsay:
"You started actually lighting things on fire. Every time you tried to light something on fire, I would take your Nalgene bottle filled with water and douse it. I kept saying, "This is dangerous!" You were mad at me because I kept trying to throw water on it."

I was infuriated.
She's using the Cup of Truth! She's wasting the truth!

Lindsay:
"You tried fighting me for the water bottle. Chasing me around the room. I was trying to keep it from you, but I was scared. I was scared you might hurt me. That was the moment I realized I couldn't do this alone. That was the moment you stopped trusting me completely.

"I said something like, 'V, I can't let you burn things in your house. You could burn the house down!' I said, 'Tear them up if you want to, but I'm not going to let you start lighting things on fire.'

"I grabbed the water bottle and would throw water anytime you would light something on fire. You got PISSED and yelled at me to stop. After the third or fourth time, you mauled me to try and get the water bottle out of my hands. Water went flying everywhere."

Lindsay is trying to put out the fire with MY Cup of Truth. She's trying to get rid of the truth! I know it isn't her fault. She doesn't realize she is impeding this process because he has her in a trance on the phone. I have to do anything and everything.

Lindsay:
"At this point, I thought it could get violent or dangerous, so I called Christine and told her to call 911. I also called 911 as soon as I got off with Christine, but was scared you would try to take my phone or get physical with me, so I wanted to make sure someone knew that I felt myself and you were in danger.

"You made a move to leave, but I stood in front of the door and said I wasn't going to let you. You grabbed some of the pictures and lighter and headed upstairs. I was terrified you were going to jump off the balcony and break your legs or light your house on fire, but I decided to stay downstairs and continue the 911 call."

I had a piece of artwork hanging in my living room. It was a rock that had been painted and mounted in a frame. The rock is painted as the face of a man with a mustache.

It represents the patriarchy. Once I get rid of it, all will be saved.

I grabbed the artwork and ran upstairs. I went to the balcony and Frisbee-threw it as hard as I could.

It is working!

Downstairs, I was burning photos inside a soup pot. It was a mix of ash and water. A messy ball of clay. When I got upstairs with everything balled up in my hands, I continued to add to it and light it on fire. I remember shaking with urgency. My hands were sore, yet the flames didn't seem to bother me while I was flying with fire. My hands were clutched so tightly around the dripping, smoking, massive ball of memories I had created. I noticed the destroyed pamphlet from my grandfather's funeral that I had torn off the fridge. I was all things. Confused, relieved, elated.

Christine:
"I called 911 when I was on the road. They were asking me questions. I walked into your courtyard, and you saw me from the balcony. You said, 'Come up here!' I walked in, and Lindsay was on the phone with 911 downstairs. She was crying."

Lindsay:
"I think it took maybe ten minutes for the police to come. In this time, I called Stephanie and the psychiatrist to let them know what happened."

I have burned all the men. My work is done.

I confidently and nervously waited for Christine to come up, with muddy ashes on my hands and a ball of wet paper clenched in my fist. I was trying not to shake.

Christine:
"When I got upstairs, I was still on the phone. You were pacing between your room and the balcony. They were asking questions like, 'What is she wearing?' I'm answering questions as I'm looking at you. You said, 'Come here.' You said, 'Take off your glasses! Get off the fucking phone!' I knew Lindsay was on the phone downstairs, so I told them I had to go.

"We sat down at the table. Your hands were full of ashes and soot, and you were holding a ball of pictures. You said, 'It's happening. It's really happening. I know what I need to do.' You were telling me how Gary was controlling your mom, and Josh (brother-in-law) was controlling your sister. You said we had to stop it at the root. I asked what the root was, and you said, 'Adam.' You brought your vision board, and you were explaining it to me. I was just trying to keep talking because I knew help was coming. I was trying to figure out where your head was. You were a bit condescending. Like you knew what was happening and I didn't, but you were going to tell me. This was weird because the night before, I got kicked out for wanting to know the truth. You were ready to tell me the truth. Then the officers showed up."

Christine has a government job. I said, "You are literally working for the man." I was referring to both her government job and as if she was serving me, believing I was God at this moment. Christine was back to being John the Baptist. A role that allows me to trust her even more when I'm thinking I am God, Jesus, or the Holy Spirit.

Christine:
"When the police came, you were playing it cool as if nothing was wrong. It was pretty funny. They had already talked to Lindsay downstairs. They were trying to figure out what this was. It looked like a domestic dispute. Your ex was downstairs crying and pictures were burned. They asked why you were burning pictures. You had no answers for the picture burning. You were just very cool and matter-of-fact. They said it was not normal to burn pictures. They asked if you slept last night. You said, 'Yup.' They looked at me confused when you said you slept. I shook my head no.

I looked at you and said they were good guys and that you could talk to them. You said, 'Isn't one of you supposed to be bad cop?' You were joking. You looked at me and said, 'I can trust them?' I said yes, and you started being more honest."

When Christine looked at me and told me they were good officers, in my mind, that meant not all men were out to get women. They were here to help me. *These aren't just men. They are my escorts. Two angels dressed as cops. They have to be undercover in order to get me out of this world.*

Christine:
"They said they would call the pert team, which is a group of people that respond to mental health issues. Every single person I have talked to since then says that PERT team is never available. Either they are way too overworked or they don't exist."

The officers were calm and so was Christine. Delusions and paranoia were secretly rolling through my head.

We have to be careful about what we were saying because our phones are tapped, and my house is tapped. In fact, the whole world is tapped. Men are controlling the phones, too. If someone is saying something they don't want others to hear over the phone, the reception will go bad, and we won't be able to hear one another.

I had to answer the cop's questions as if I were Veronica but had to think as God. That way, the men that I thought were listening to our conversation wouldn't realize what I was really saying. For example, when they asked for my address, I used "Veronica's actual address." I did not say something like, "I am everywhere." It was hard to go back and forth in my mind, and sometimes I was left with no words, and Christine would have to interject.

Christine:
"One of the officers said, 'Your friends are concerned. We don't really know what is going on here. Would you be willing to go to the hospital? If nothing is wrong, we will bring you right back.' You said, 'Okay.'"

They gave me two hospital choices. One had the word "Mercy" in it, which is the one I chose. *I choose this because it makes me think of Jesus' mercy.* The street name of the hospital happened to be Zion, which is a place referenced in the bible, so in my religiously delusional state, I readily went along with it all.

Christine:
"We tried to find your shoes. Apparently, you didn't want Lindsay to find your shoes. You wanted me to find your shoes."

Lindsay was downstairs, and I thought she had been brainwashed by my psychiatrist to join the dark side. I had no shoes on before I left, and Christine said, "Do you want to get your sandals?" I immediately thought of the bible quote John 1:27. "Even he who comes after me, the thong of whose sandal I am not worthy to untie." Lindsay had gone upstairs to get my shoes and plopped them on the floor. Not sandals. I just looked at her. I needed Christine to put the sandals on my feet. I needed the shoes to come from her and no one else.

I was not going to pick up the shoes from Lindsay. In my mind at the time, it would have meant I was accepting something from the darkness. Once Christine pointed them out, I put them on. Lindsay said. "So, because I brought them to you, you don't want them?"

Lindsay was wiped out, and even though it wasn't "me" putting her through this, it's hard not to be left with the shame and guilt of knowing that regardless of mania, it was "me" who caused a lot of trauma to the people closest to me.

Christine:
"I asked Lindsay if she wanted to go with you and I would drive or the other way around. She said, 'Nope. I'm out. I can't.' I tapped in."

Lindsay:
"I was a frazzled ball of nerves at that point and decided to go home to get some sleep rather than go to the ER since I knew you'd be safe now. You were mad at me anyway, so I felt my presence would do more harm than good."

As they escorted me out to the cop car, they asked about my music career. Small talk. I talked about my solo career. The conversation triggered a series of thoughts. *Wait. Salvation isn't through faith (Lindsay), hope (me) and love (Jason Mraz). All along it is just me! I am all three! Much like the trinity.*

Christine:
"We jumped in the back of the cop car and joked a little bit. I told him you were the nicest person he would probably meet this week."

I am safe but the cop car is tapped. I just need to be quiet. They are driving me to the beach. This time, I do not have to die. All of my friends are going to be at the beach to thank me for opening the gates of heaven on Earth for all of eternity.

My lips pressed together intentionally with smudged glasses on my face, Christine took this selfie:

You can see that I'm somewhere else. A bit confused but hopeful. Mainly confused and processing.

Before I started burning the pictures and was calm, Lindsay had said the phrase, "He can't see without his glasses." It is an inside joke we say to each other, and it was just a throwaway comment. *She was giving me a clue. Men can only tell that I am God if they are wearing glasses. In order to protect my identity, I have to keep my glasses on.*

From that point I was very concerned with keeping my glasses on.

53

Weirdest. Surgery. Ever.

Christine:
"It worked out well because had you gone to the ER voluntarily it would have taken a while. With the officers we just got in. We got there at 8:50, and at 9, beds would be available. The four of us were standing around. They were bringing people in, and at one point, you went to talk to someone. I said, 'No, she's okay.' You were going to save somebody. The officers didn't get it. They knew something was off, but you weren't super off. You were still so nice. Not violent. Not talking too much nonsense. You were pretty quiet. In that state, you want to help. They got you a bed and a gown. The officers left."

I walked into the ER and looked for all the women. *They are more in charge now. The men answer to the women? My efforts worked! The new world is here and women are taking the lead role. It's a new dawn! It's a new day!*

I watched for the men with glasses from the corner of my eye and made sure they wouldn't look into my eyes. We got a bed in no time, and I laid down. I started feeling a little scared.

I lie there waiting. I was calm. Christine was with me. The curtain was closed. *I am safe at the moment.*

Christine:
"You were okay. You wanted to see the documents they had on you. Not totally out of it. The ER doctor came, and he was a douche. He was my least favorite person we met all day. He asked, 'What is going on here?' And you said, 'Well, I'm bipolar.' He said, 'Yeah, but why are you here?' You said, 'Well. These are the meds I'm on.' You couldn't answer the questions, and he kept pushing. Finally, he looked at me and said, 'Can you answer?' He asked if you had thoughts of hurting yourself or others? You said, 'Yes.' He sent in for a psych eval."

In retrospect, it surprised me that I said that I was in danger of hurting others or myself because I never thought that. I believe my motive was to get to the ICU in order to "save" people.

Christine:
"You asked me to read the patients' rights. I tried to read them like a bedtime story. Trying to lull you to sleep. I avoided any trigger words."

On one of the papers a nurse gave me, it had some jargon, but at the bottom, it said something about transgendered people/people going through sex changes. I have no idea what context it was because my head felt so mixed.

I am going to have a sex change. My dad just got out of surgery in New York. They are going to do surgery on me with no anesthesia, so that I will look like my dad. That way people won't realize it was a woman who saved the world. It will be more believable.

I'm not the only person who comes to the ER with delusions that staff will be performing some type of procedure.

Alex B:
"(I thought I was) Superman. I thought I was a genetic experiment in the hospital. I thought they were working on me because I had super radioactive powers. There was radioactivity in the room, and I was resistant to it."

The ER is a hotbed for delusions.

Alex B:
"I had delusions that there were famous people around me at the hospital. People like Snoop Dogg. He was outside the window driving around. I thought my counselor was Tom from Rage Against the Machine."

A nurse came in.

She is collecting data on me and trying to confirm that I am, in fact, Jesus. All the women on the unit realize I'm here. They can see me with or without glasses.

I started thinking about my sister, Steph, who was with my dad in New York who was just out of surgery. Then I started thinking about "Star Wars" again. *Luke I am your father…it means something. Wait! My father is THE Father.*

My Dad is GOD! I am his son and Steph is The Holy Spirit. They are going to be on their way to save me, but in the meantime, I am going to have surgery. My heart is racing, but I can't lead on. I am scared. I have to calm myself. This is all for the greater good. I will suffer, but it won't be long.

54

Push Push Swipe

I believed I passed them one by one.

One of these tests happened when I had my phone. I had texts saved from people.

It's judgment time. I have to delete the texts from the people who are not worthy to share in the delights of Heavenly eternity.

One by one, I deleted people for one reason or another. *Now they have been sent to hell.* A nurse came in right as I finished. *Her coming in means that I've passed the test.*

Noelle came by. She happened to work as a music therapist at the hospital. She is another person I trust and feel safe with. My thoughts went back to the patient's rights. I asked Christine to hand them to me and was frantically trying to memorize parts of it, but I couldn't think clearly. *I need to know my rights before I have them violated.*

Noelle said, "Hey, let me know if they are taking care of you because I have some pull in here…no, I don't."

Her sarcasm didn't translate in my mind. I thought she was being serious. It made me feel like she was being oppressed by the men in the hospital. I reacted.

Christine:
"You shot out of bed and lost it. You were screaming, and you were trying to get through the curtain. As soon as you got out, you were screaming really loud. You pushed all the shit down from the counter. 'Push, Push, Swipe.' I distinctly remember. Thank God Noelle was there. We stayed out of the way. One guy said, 'Are you serious?!' He was so pissed you threw stuff down. He ended up being very nice."

I remember looking around as everyone froze and stared at me. I started screaming as hard as I could. Everyone looked shocked.

Christine:
"The security guard came, and you hunkered down, ready to hulk out and hit somebody. One of the officers that took us in was back, and he said, 'I don't want to hurt you.' He kept saying that. I averted my eyes because. I didn't want to see them take you down. Then you started singing, 'There Is Hope' really loud."

I need to get to the ICU to save everyone! It is all so clear now. There will be a piano in the ICU, and my songs will free them. I have to sing as loud as I can, so they know I am coming. I must sing louder! 'There is hope in the emptiest hole! There is hope when there's nowhere to go! There Is Hoooooope!'

As I was tackled to the ground, my face hit the ground and my glasses bounced off of my face. I started cry-singing my song, "There Is Hope." Without my glasses, I felt totally exposed. It was my protection against others seeing who I really was.

Now everyone knows I have come back down to earth. They are going to want to crucify me.

Christine:
"You went limp when they handcuffed you."

You must surrender, like a lamb being led to slaughter.

Christine:
"They transferred you to a bed, and gave you a shot of Haldol. It was around 10:30. Then you were out the rest of the day."

All at once, just as the storm came with no warning, it left with no warning. A few people had to carry me by arms and legs to the bed. That is the last thing I remember about being in the ER.

Christine was by my side. She didn't go home until 10:30 p.m.

Christine:
"You got up once to go to the bathroom. You had already peed the bed. They got you a new setup, and I told you to let me know when you had to go to the bathroom. I just sat there until two or three when Nikki and Janet got there. I went out to get food and came back.

Nikki, Janet, (my friends), and I were there, and finally, the psych people came. This was around 5:00 p.m. They were called in around 9:30 that morning. They kept telling me it was because you were out and needed to wait 'til you woke up, but then other people just told me they were backed up. I can't even imagine if they hadn't knocked you out if you had to wait seven hours for a psych eval. A doctor talked to you, and we showed her 'The Plan.' She was super nice. She transferred you to another private room that was in a psych area with its own staff. Fewer rooms. It was great. That is when you woke up, and Michele, Kristen, and Janet were there."

The first thing I recall was when I was in the private room. I felt pretty much back to normal, as if nothing had happened. I remember opening my eyes and seeing people around me. My thought was, "it happened again…I can't believe this happened again."

he said he was on hour twelve. He said he didn't have a choice because they don't get paid very well. Twelve hours was typical, but he had done longer. He said, "I do it because I care."

55

Small World

Any fear I had seemed to melt as we got inside. The hospital floor was low stimulus and had a relaxing quality. I got my vitals taken and walked down the hallway to my room. Halfway down the hall, a teenage boy was walking the other way. I looked up.

It was one of my guitar students from the school where I taught lessons.

It was such an unbelievable coincidence that I had no time to process any of what just happened. There were twelve patients in an ICU unit in San Diego, and we were in the same one at the same time. To put this in perspective, San Diego County alone is the size of Connecticut. What. Were. The. Chances. Why did it happen this way?

When I got to him, I stopped and said, "What happened?" He was not able to answer me. He was very disoriented, flat affect, rigid, and slow movements. Some of it may have had to do with the medications he was on. In groups, he would very calmly say, "I'm going to kill all the men in this room." At one point, he looked at me and said, "Am I an age?"

Mental illness is all around. It doesn't always express itself, so you can't always tell. It could be your neighbor or your childhood best friend. It could be the person you sit across from at work. It could be your guitar student.

We didn't talk much. I knew I needed to focus on my recovery when I found myself wanting to comfort him. It was a lesson I needed to learn. And relearn. And relearn. A lesson that, once I dug deeper, I found the real bottom: If I care too much for others, I can neglect myself. Because in the end, I'm not really worth all of this. Focus out and I will run out of time for myself.

I was inside while my loved ones were on the outside, concerned. Becca and I still hadn't been totally established as partners at this time and not everyone had her number. Once I stopped trusting her and asked her to leave, she was not in the loop as much as my long-standing friends were.

Becca:
"After you'd been hospitalized, I felt like I was in the dark. Everything went silent. I'm sure it was only a few days but it felt like a lifetime. I remember Christine eventually called to give me an update, and I felt like I could finally take a breath. At the end of the conversation, Christine asked how I was doing. I don't remember my exact response, but I do know that I was trying really hard not to cry. That's when she said something that gave me enough hope to get through the whole experience. She said, "She always comes back. I know it's scary, and it doesn't seem like it now, but she always comes back." I held onto those words tighter than anything, especially while you were in the hospital. I held onto them on days I didn't get to see you and when I had no way to know how you were doing."

"She always comes back."

56

Meet the ICU Crew

Overall, I was doing well, and the best part was, I was of sound mind. There was such a variety of people around me in the hospital. I found it fascinating, inspiring, and disheartening.

There was a man there who had just been diagnosed with schizophrenia and he was also in the armed services and suffered from PTSD. He said he was glad he finally got a diagnosis because he knew something was off. He was also suffering from depression. His face was tight, and he had flat affect. It felt as though I could see him caving in.

My roommate was sweet, but I could tell she had a rough side. She would change her clothes about five times a day. I never knew her diagnosis, but she did seem paranoid. When I got to the unit, she was nice to me. They were all nice to me.

Another girl was about twenty. She had drug-induced schizophrenia. She had some odd behaviors that looked like severe OCD, but I think she was probably having delusions. She would talk very fast about things that didn't make sense. We would be talking about something, and she would try to make a point, but the point would be about a completely unrelated story. The stories were usually about aliens and she always carried a deck of cards with her. During our time outside, she and I were sitting across from one another at a table. She looked at me and said, "Pick a card." I picked a six of hearts. She smiled at me and said, "You just got six million dollars in your bank account." She believed it. I did a fist pump in the air and said, "Yes!" I didn't want to feed into it but I wanted her to feel good at the moment. Why not join her world for a moment?

Every night we got to listen to music for about an hour in the main room. She would dance to every song. It didn't look exactly like dancing sometimes. She would watch her reflection in the window when she danced. I admired it all because she did not care what other people thought of her. She may not have had the ability to care. Also, she kept trying to give me her extra clothes.

Another man was addicted to heroin and alcohol. He had been in and out of wards for a while. One day, he got a call in the unit from his wife saying she wanted a divorce. He didn't know how to stop it. He said he used when he had downtime. It was hard to be home alone because he knew he could use.

Another person about my age was very slow moving. He had flat affect and his mouth hung open. I assumed he was totally out of it until music time one night. The song, "Hotline Bling" by Drake came on. The whole room of people seemed to light up. Everyone started moving and perking up a bit more. He was sitting on a couch, and the minute it started, he got a tiny side smile which caused me to smile. He faintly mouthed the chorus. Next up was, "Now watch me whip, watch me nae nae." He put his arms above his head and did the upper body dance moves, but he did it on a tamer, slower level with micromovements. He looked much like an old animatronic character from a run-down amusement park ride.

If I thought this guy was just out of it because of his mental illness, I can't imagine what people who don't have a mental illness thought. We had group therapy one day, and he was there. At one point, I said, "Do people treat you differently because you're heavily medicated?" He looked at me with his eyes half open, mouth hung open, and shook his head, "Yes."

We had morning and evening check-ins. We would have to rate how we felt, what our goals were for the day, and tell if we met our goals from the day before. It was dinnertime check-in, and we were having tuna casserole for dinner. When it was his turn, he said, "I'm feeling like I want tuna casserole, and my goal is to have tuna casserole." It was hard to tell if he was trying to make a joke or not, but I definitely smiled. His nails were long and dirty, and his clothes were wrinkled. For me, and possibly for him too, self-care goes out the window when so much is being thrown into the window.

Another girl was probably in her mid-twenties. I think she had pretty severe schizophrenia. She had big movements and had a hard time sitting still in one place. It looked like psychomotor agitation. She would interrupt conversations, but it didn't seem like she even knew conversations were happening. The only time she would be calm was during art time. She would still move around but not as much.

One day I was walking down the hall just to do something and keep my heart rate up. I passed her room, and she was throwing things out of her cabinets. Her room was chaotic. She screamed, "I'M LOOKING FOR SOMETHING!" I watched for a moment. She was not searching while she threw things. She was just throwing things in all sorts of directions.

During outside time she would smoke her cigarettes fast and pace back and forth. One day she paced by me, looked up, and said, "I like your sweatshirt." She had never acknowledged me before or after that. It was as if she was living in two worlds at once all the time.

Another man was my age and looked just like my cousin. He was tall and lanky but looked strong. Pale skin, fiery eyes, still face. I didn't know how to take him. He never lashed out, and he was altogether pretty quiet, but there was something about him that looked like it could get very angry quickly. He had been in the ICU for over a month, and he wanted out.

During group one day, he was loudly eating chips. The therapist told him there was no food allowed in group and to please stop. He stared at her intently and slowly brought one chip at a time up to his mouth. She would give him a warning after each chip. I was amused. When he spoke, his voice was loud and static. Not much inflection.

The staff was good. I had no problems. but there were moments when some people were spoken to like second-class citizens.

The ward consisted of a hallway about 100 feet long, with approximately ten bedrooms, a kitchen area, and a room with couches where therapies would also take place. I did tricep and bicep exercises and lots of pushups in my room to keep busy and focused. Art time was my time to try to get it all out. I was focusing on my recovery as much as I could.

Before I knew it, they had a bed for me in another unit, and off I went. Before I left, I asked the dancing girl if I could pick a card. I drew a nine of clubs. Nine million metaphorical dollars in my bank account, and I'm out. It felt like I had graduated. Had I known what it would be like, however, I would have asked to be held back.

57

Music: The Real Hero

It was sort of comical how close the other unit was. We took about twenty steps out of the unit, and the other unit was right in front of us. This unit is usually a mix of mood disorder and chemical dependency. I was the only person on the unit there with a diagnosis of mental illness sans chemical dependency and/or alcohol addiction. Everyone else was there for either alcohol and drug reasons or eating disorders. I do understand that if someone is using, they might be trying to manage their very own mental struggles without help.

Right as I walked through the double doors of the new unit, I felt a little lighter. Our art room was outside the unit, and there were a ton more options in terms of art supplies.

Our lunchroom was also off the unit, and we got choices of what to eat and drink. In the ICU, the lunchroom was also the art room, which was also the TV room and also the therapy room. There were no options for meals in the ICU. What you see is what you get.

Another thing I noted in the ICU was the way the soap dispenser in the shower was mounted in my bathroom. The dispenser was slightly left of the knob that turns on the shower. Because the shower was already small, I had to bend to the side to shower.

What might seem like an inconvenience in a stable mind can be a mindf*ck in the unstable mind, whether it causes agitation or makes you think someone is controlling you by putting it in your way. After the three ICU-to-open-unit experiences I have had, I realize it is all backward. They treat people in the ICU like the coach class in an airplane.

To me, it feels as though the more incompetent a patient appears; the less respect others have for that patient. If a patient doesn't seem to have agency, a staff member notices and their attitude, and the way they talk with a patient changes.

I went into one of the main rooms on the unit and just observed my environment. I was socializing and making the best of this situation. I remember feeling a bit on edge but my mind felt clear. I felt like I was completely in the room as Veronica. No delusions. No paranoia. I leaned back in my chair and looked to my right. I saw exactly what I needed; a guitar was leaning on the wall in the corner. I got tears in my eyes, quickly leaned over, and picked it up.

The first night on the unit ended up being a sing-along night. I played songs and people requested songs. It was a mutually beneficial situation. While in the unit, I wrote three songs with the help of that guitar. One of the patients would frequently ask me to play. If he ever saw I was playing, he would lie next to me in the hall or main room, close his eyes, and listen.

I wouldn't be surprised if that guitar was the reason I was out of the hospital in eight days and not ten or eleven.

I had my eye on the prize: Getting out. Not just getting out. Getting out safely. What I had learned from my last episode was that getting out early, while enticing, was not the way. That if I felt in any way unstable, I should just stay and wait. The unit provided us with notebooks if we wanted them.

I drew in the notebooks, wrote lyrics, wrote things I would overhear people say, took notes from groups, and vented about staff and patients.

I kind of felt like an undercover journalist during some points. I realized that a firsthand, lucid account of a hospital stay could benefit others and to put a lot of it into this book. Then I hid the notebook in between clothes at night and questioned if I was becoming paranoid again. Halfway through my stay I handed off my journal to Lindsay during visitation. I then began another journal and around the end of my stay I gave it to Noelle during visitation.

58

Why Don't You Cry about It?

This was my favorite hospital of all three. Oddly, a big part was the carpet on the floor. It gave the illusion of a home and not a hospital. The staff was great too. All but one. I will call her Melinda, the mental health worker. It seemed evident that Melinda hated her job. She would boss around other staff as she sat around.

Melinda did not like me, but I was not special. She didn't like anyone. She had to check the temperature and blood pressure of each patient. I was a ball of nerves one day, and she was checking vitals and writing the numbers down for each patient. Out of curiosity, I wanted to know how fast my heart was beating. When the machine stopped, it said my heart rate was 116 bpm. Not crazy fast, but also much faster than the at-rest state of 60 bpm. She didn't say anything. She looked at me and said, "You aren't sick, are you?" And didn't take my temperature. "Next."

This may seem like such a little thing. Who cares if she didn't document my temperature? I wasn't sick. But if she was skimping on this, what else was she skimping on? What else is everyone skimping on?

One day we went down to lunch as usual. Most days, I just kept to myself or talked to one person. I was done with my food on this day and in a conversation. I don't remember what the conversation was about. Then there was a moment of silence. I felt like I was going to cry. It came from nowhere. I put my head down and clasped my hands around my mouth. Someone tried to console me by putting their hand on my shoulder. I said, "I don't need to be consoled!"

It was good timing because we were all about to be led back to our unit. I walked at a faster pace, so I could get to our unit. My hand was still around my mouth like I was kidnapping myself.

When I got in the unit, walked down the hallway, got in my room, closed the door, got on my bed, and grabbed my pillow. I just started screaming. I wasn't trying to scream, I was trying to cry. I scream-cried into the pillow. It seemed each time I took a breath, I would get louder. My vocal cords clashed together until I became hoarse. My eyes bulged forward and I cried until I couldn't. I made sure every last bit was out. I took a long moment flat on my face, "I'm here again somehow. It happened again…" the sentences looped in my head. I got myself together and left my room. I was hoping this wouldn't give anyone a reason to keep me in the hospital longer. But in reality, if I had such a big emotional outpouring, I probably needed to be in the hospital longer.

I remember the looks on the other patient's faces when it was all going down. They looked scared, startled, and in disbelief.

I was just trying to keep it together. I wanted to explain that I had bipolar and that this might be part of that. I didn't feel understood here.

I grabbed my journal and wrote as fast as I could:

1/14/16
"I'm feeling on the edge. I'm trying to keep it together. I am not going to give up. I'm not going to give up. Not giving up. Not giving up. Not giving up. Not giving up. Not giving up. I am strong. I am calm. I am peaceful. I am steady. I am present. I am here. I can do this. I can do this. I can do this. I can do this. I am here. I can do this. I can do this. I can. I am positive. I can I can. I am here. I can. I can. I can. I am here. I am calm. I"

For some reason, I ended with "I." This may have been around the time visitation was starting. There were a few times visitors came and I was deep in writing or drawing.

I remember I felt so isolated. No one on this unit understood me. Worse than that, they would make fun of the people in the ICU. One girl used the word "psycho," and I looked at her and said, "It isn't right to use that word. I'm one of those psychos." She got up and left. I don't blame her for leaving. It's hard to understand things you've never experienced.

At one point during my stay, the ICU alarm went off. It was the girl who had been most out of it at the ICU. The girl that had been throwing papers. A patient made a joke saying he hoped she wasn't going to shank us. A statement that, to me, said more about him than it did her. When the mental health workers got back in the office, one of them said, "She's just trying to start shit again."

It baffles me that mental health workers, people who have actually been trained in this area, do not understand that those behaviors are being driven by delusions, paranoia, hallucinations, depression, anxiety. In short, chemicals.

I felt like I was hitting my boiling point. Yes, I was balanced in terms of being lucid. But I was mad, I was scared, I was hopeful, I was feeling many feelings all at once and it was hard to navigate while keeping my composure. Melinda was still at work; negativity was swirling around me. I had to use my coping skills:

1. Food. I needed something in my stomach. I was a shaky mess and tears were sliding down my face. I grabbed some chips in the pantry and walked out to the hallway. I sat with my back against the wall. I couldn't get the chips open because I was shaking so much. I pulled harder and a fanfare of chips danced out of the bag and landed on the floor.
2. Humor. A nurse saw the whole thing go down. I got on my hands and knees and said, "I'm literally picking up the pieces." The nurse told me she could throw them away. I bit into a chip, and she said it was gross. I said I had no shame.
3. Music. I finished the chips and grabbed the guitar. I went into my room, sat on the chair, rested my forehead on the guitar, closed my eyes, and played. My lip was quivering, and I was catching my breath. I played until I stopped crying and brought the guitar back to the main room.

59

Coming Alive Again

It was time for us to line up to leave for art therapy. When I got in the line, I saw one of the guys from ICU. My heart did a little jump for joy. I said, "Hey. It's so good to see you." It was the lanky man who ate chips during group. He let a small smile peek out. When we got to art therapy, he got a piece of paper and a pen. He just wrote out, "Let me out of here." We were listening to music, and he would sing certain words out loud and then get quiet again. I looked at him and said, "Are you reading into these lyrics?" He said "yes." I told him, "You don't have to." It looked like that put him at ease.

Outside time and gym time were great. I needed to get a lot of energy out. During gym time, I would just throw a ball against the wall as hard as I could. I would switch from one activity to the next, knowing we wouldn't have long. Two people came to the gym from the ICU one day. When the staff opened the doors to the gym, they looked like kids in a candy store. "Wow." One of them said, they both ran around, played basketball, and lifted. They got a lot of energy out.

During outside activity we would go on the tennis court that also had basketball hoops. I played tennis with some people one day. I remember how good It felt to be out of breath. A ball came sailing my way, and I sprinted across the court. The sudden movement woke my mind up. I felt alive. I reached out and hit it. As I swung, I yelled, "I'm not going to give up!!" I said it again in my mind. "I'm not going to give up." I ran as hard as I could and lunged at the ball, hitting it just enough to get it back over the net. "I DID IT!" I started mouthing the phrase as we continued to play. "I'm not going to give up. I'm not going to give up." I smiled, tears in my eyes.

Once during tennis, a patient said, "This feels like a resort." In my head, I thought, "Is that what you are getting out of your recovery? Like this is some spa for you?" Later in the week, I had asked that same guy what area of town he lived in. He said, "I don't live in any area of town. I'm homeless." I had forgotten that some of these people were going to get discharged back into their real and miserable lives. This was his resort. This was his chance to have something more.

60

Sorry I'm Acting Like a Dick

There were groups in which I called the therapists out while they were leading the group. This is not something I would typically do. So, while I was sound of mind, I was also saying whatever was on my mind.

I was excited that there were music therapists on staff. When the first session began, I looked at the music therapist's name tag. It did not say MT-BC (music therapy board certified). I didn't know if she was board certified, and it made me upset, knowing how much you have to study in order to be certified myself. In the music therapy handbook, under the code of ethics, a music therapist cannot practice without this certification. She was explaining who she was and getting the group started. I interrupted her and said, "Are you board certified?" Everyone looked at her. She seemed caught off guard. She was not. As a music therapist, it didn't sit well with me. I'm not sure how she could even call it music therapy without having a background in it. Most people who don't know what music therapy is think it's just a bunch of people listening to songs and feeling better.

It was drilled into me in college that you cannot be in practice without certification.

In another music therapy group, a lot of people came. The therapist brought a bunch of drums, but after seeing so many people decided to do something else. I probably would have done that too. Right out of the gate, I asked if he was board certified. He said, "Yes. I am also NMT (Neurologic Music Therapy) certified." That's the type of music therapy I was trained in. He started out group saying, "So, why does rhythm move our bodies? No one really knows." I interrupted and said, "Actually, rhythm stimulates the motor neurons." He said something along the lines of, "Well, that is what some might think. I like to think it has something to do with water molecules." He pulled out his iPod. He would play a song and then say, "What does this song bring up for you?" I stood up and walked out.

This is, in fact, something I might do as a music therapist. Playing familiar songs can bring up a lot of emotions for many people. In an environment where people have literal mood regulation difficulties, something as simple as a song can really trigger a stressful event. It can also allow people to open up and talk. During this stay, I didn't have the bandwidth to find out if this intervention was going to be productive or not. Now that I've been on the "other side of therapy," I can see how a lot of interventions I may have done too, were maybe not the best idea. We were all in crisis. Many of us feeling fragile. Some of us delusional, believing the song lyrics were actually about us. Reading into the lyrics. If I were to lead a group of people in this population again, I would most likely do unfamiliar instrumental music or have participants create their own instrumental music with simple instruments.

The cognitive group was led by an older woman. It was a mood disorder group and a lot of the people from ICU were there. She started out group by showing us a deck of cards with different questions on it. There was a wild card in the deck. She also had a fake million-dollar bill. In a voice one might imagine an adult to use for a preschooler, she said, "Okaaaaay, whoever picks the wild card gets the money. It's a million-dollar bill for someone lucky! Who is this on the million-dollar bill? It is a president." I interrupted and said, "Do you think this is age appropriate?"

It was blunt, which I am not generally in a totally stable state. And it wasn't age appropriate, it made me feel small.

Without skipping a beat, she started talking about anger management. She asked why I was in the hospital during group. I told her I had a manic episode and that I thought the men in the pictures at my house were controlling the women. She got Freudian and started talking about sexual abuse and domestic violence. I told her it was a delusion, and she looked at me as if she'd never even heard the word.

I started realizing that no matter the amount of training, the only thing that would really help someone see Bipolar I would be for them to have Bipolar I.

Another therapist kept checking his watch for the time. He ended right as the hour was over. He would say, "Does everyone understand?" And without pause, would then say, "Okay, good." He would address everyone's questions— Everyone but one woman who came from the older adult unit that day. I think she had some sort of developmental delay as well. Possibly a traumatic brain injury (TBI), but I don't know. She talked very loud and in fragmented sentences. Her face would contort. She seemed very sweet. I had seen her in a few groups. When she kept trying to ask questions, the therapist would say, "We will talk about that later" or "Not right now." He never got to her questions.

I remember walking by a gray box in the hallway. It was a comment box. I had put five or six comments in the comment box. All constructive criticism. There was a section that said, "Check if you would like to be contacted once this has been reviewed." I checked that box on all of them, and I still haven't gotten a call. I never will.

61

The Sunrays

Some therapists in the unit were excellent and had a lot of compassion. I remember one in particular. It was a process group. There was one man who was there for depression. His voice was quiet, and I remember thinking, "He looks like a shell of what he probably really is." He said he felt stupid and never knew what to talk about. I totally understood where he was coming from, as I had been there at times in the past. The therapist asked the group, "What could he talk about?" I said, "After group, we could talk about puppies." So, we did and he did. It reminded me of my own depressions. How alone he must have felt. How incompetent and burdensome he must have been feeling. It felt good to feel like a support for that moment. To take my mind off of my own current problems.

An art therapist on staff made a difference too. She must have been a sub or maybe weekend staff, as we only had her once. She had us make grounding bracelets with letters and images that we could string onto our bracelets. I put a bunch of brown beads on it to represent the earth. I put one red bead on it to represent love, and one blue bead to represent peace.

She kept a calm environment in the room and would comment on other's work. People started talking about their kids, their parents. They started opening up. To finish my bracelet, I spelled the words, "I am here." I stared at the bracelet until my eyes stung. I had to believe it. A stream of tears drifted down my face.

62

"Agitated"

The days in the unit were structured well. I knew what to expect and there was enough to do but not too much to do. After the visitations were over, I got to relax and get ready for bed. Many nights I would lie awake thinking, "Did I get my meds tonight?" Night after night, staff did not go to rooms for medication checks. If I weren't a proactive person or a person who had my mind at this point, who knows? Would they have even come to get me if I hadn't stood in the medication line? Had I been forgetting to get medications in the morning and night?

During my first meeting to discuss medications, the psychiatrist on staff asked how I ended up in the ICU. When I told him I was knocking things down in the hospital, he seemed surprised, and somewhat skeptical. As if it was a behavior. "Why would you do that?" I told him I needed to get to the ICU to save the patients because I thought I was Jesus. He said, "So you threw things around to get into the ICU?" As if I had any say in the matter at the time. As if psychosis is logical.

Sweet as he was, he went against my primary psychiatrist's orders, saying what he wanted to do was a better idea. I wanted to speak up. I had been seeing my primary for over four years. Thankfully, two days later, the weekend psychiatrist was in, and I broke down in her office. I felt like I wasn't being heard. She said she would put me on the doses my psychiatrist wanted. I told her I didn't think I was getting the medications, only to find out they were also giving me the wrong doses in the morning—150 mg instead of 200 mg. I told her I was concerned, so she approached the medication desk. She asked the medication nurse if I had been getting my medications, and he said, "Yes." She asked to see the chart and sure enough, there were days of no documentation on getting one of my medications. I told the medication nurse it was unsettling not knowing if I was getting the right doses at the right times. When I looked at my chart the next morning, he had written a note on the date of our interaction that just said, "Agitated."

One day, we got a new medication nurse. She had said this was her first time "flying solo." She asked staff if she should roll the medication cart down the hall if someone wasn't coming out to get medications, and the answer she got was, "Some people do that."

It took a long time to get medications because the organization of the med cabinet was atrocious. Each med type was in a different baggie like the Ziplocs you can get at the grocery store. The staff would have to file through the sea of baggies to find each medication. Then they would have to open the seal of the individually wrapped pills in order to administer them. I found myself trying to watch like a hawk by reading the tiny, individually wrapped packages. I didn't want them to think I was micromanaging. I was just nervous.

During med time one night, I was looking at the medication they pulled out. It was not one of mine. I said, "That isn't the right med." To which they said, "Oops. Someone made a boo-boo."

I had openly talked about the medication issues and brought it up to mental health workers. During night medications on the day I brought it up, Melinda came into a group therapy session and made an announcement. "Okay, if you haven't taken your meds, come grab a number." Sticky notes with numbers written with Sharpie. This was the first and last time it was done.

This was never protocol before. I kept taking notes in the therapy session and had forgotten to get a number. I remembered as I left the group.

I walked down the hallway to where the med line was. There were two people in line and Melinda was nowhere to be found. I wasn't about to track her down for a number she scrawled on a Post-it. No one else was in line behind me.

I was second in line for about fifteen minutes. The patient that was at the med desk was asking for her PRNs.[1] She was in the unit for drug abuse. When the med nurse gave her the med, she claimed it fell on the floor, and that part of it dissolved in her hand. She swore she didn't swallow it. She clearly swallowed it and wanted another. This went on for a while. I was annoyed at first but then saw how sad it was.

Finally, the woman in front of me was up, and the med nurse told her to wait. The med nurse proceeded to go into the nurse's station and chat with the other nurses. It was clear she wasn't doing a thing. She did this for about five minutes and strolled back.

Now I was next in line and waiting. I had nowhere else to be, so I realized there wasn't much urgency. Melinda walked

---

[1] PRN medication means medication that is administered as needed. The time of medication administration is determined by the resident's need. https://www.lawinsider.com/dictionary/prn-medication

down the hall and stopped when she got to me. "Did you get a number?" I told her I hadn't. "Oh, well, then you will have to wait at the back of the line." The back of the line that did not exist. I readily agreed with her. I felt like she had some sort of weird power which made me question how lucid I was feeling. It felt like a paranoia that was warranted. I didn't want her to write anything in her notes that could keep me in the hospital longer.

I really felt a night and day difference when Melinda was there. I couldn't believe the weight of one person who really didn't seem to care about their job or how it was done. Looking back, I wonder how much of my own emotions played into how awful she really was.

63

Hope Rings True

When I arrived at the hospital on the first day at the ICU, I had to put a bracelet and ring in a baggie for the staff to keep. I was told I could now access them on the open unit. Another crying bout came on strong, and I started to panic. I took long strides down the hallway and approached a very sweet nurse. Through my tears, I said, "Can I please go get my ring? Please?" I know it was a special request but she could see I really needed it. "Okay, let's go," she said.

We walked down the hallway to where personal belongings were kept. She found the Ziploc bag and pulled out the ring. She placed it in my hand, and I started crying again. I put it on and stared at the word that was engraved in it: Hope. "There is hope. There is hope." I repeated out loud to myself. I knew hope was the thing to navigate me through this hospital stay.

I always looked forward to the evening visitations more than anything. Visitation lasted for an hour and a half, and Christine and Lindsay coordinated the visits. After each visitation, my friends would ask who I would like to see the following day. Some people were repeats as they were people

I felt grounded around. This hospital stay felt a little different in that some of these patients did, in fact, have a visitor or two. The difference may have been that most of these patients weren't there because of a mental health crisis. They were there for drug and alcohol addiction. Although mental health issues and using can be closely linked.

One visit in particular gave me a very good laugh. My friend Kristen came into the main visitation room. A mental health worker passed by and made a comment about my guitar playing, and Kristen said, "Yeah, isn't she insane?"

She got really quiet, and then, all at once, we burst into laughter. It felt so good to laugh hard. Sometimes, I would start to cry mid-sentence during visitations, and my friends would hold my hand or put their arms around me. They sat with me in silence, they made jokes, they talked about what they had been up to. So often my friends knew what I needed and when I needed it. They just let me be where I was.

During one visit, my friend, Michele, brought me a blank book. She had drawn pictures of flowers and such in random parts of the book that I could color in. This book was my saving grace for the remainder of my stay. I looked at the front cover and wrote, "The lessons I have learned." It was complete with illustrations of myself in different situations. I was able to come up with twenty-one different lessons I had learned while being in the hospital. It felt good to focus on something. If I look close enough, I can see how pain has shaped me into something different. I feel like the lessons are always there. It's up to me to make them into something.

64

Hide AND Seek

During visitations, I would usually sit in the hallway away from everyone in the main room visiting. There was a lot of noise and one night, a few patients were sitting in the hall together with no visitors. I was sitting with my friends. We were laughing hard about something. I always had more energy when they left. As one patient passed, she said, "Hello, perfect." It broke my heart for her more than anything. She hadn't had visitors or support and she seemed so broken inside. If only she knew how imperfect I was feeling. In a weird way, it validated that I "appeared" to be on the right track.

Toby came to visit one day. She took over my clients while I was in the hospital and while I was recovering. She sat down next to me and said, "What do I tell your clients and their families?" I said, "Tell them I had a manic episode."

Maybe it sounds like an obvious thing to tell because it's what happened. But as I was telling her what to say, I thought it was too unprofessional. But it was the truth, and I wanted them to know that. If it were a car accident, it wouldn't have been a question of what to tell them.

I realized then by hiding my illness, I would be broadcasting to the world that it is not okay to have bipolar. It is certainly okay to have bipolar. It is even okay to talk about it as a therapist in a setting in which it holds therapeutic value for a client. It can bridge the gap. Being open can allow another person to open up.

Some of us hide the things we are somewhat ashamed of. We hide the things we feel we must protect. We hide the things we think other people would frown upon. When I open up to people, it is generally easier than I expect it to be.

Days in the hospital came and went. I stayed three more days than expected, as I was still cycling. I didn't let it discourage me too much. I knew if I was released, I could possibly relapse back into something. It was safer inside. Because I was on the most expensive health insurance plan (the only plan that behavioral health is covered by) a lot of my stay was paid for. As a white, privileged individual, I have been able to navigate med expenses, hospital, relapses. To put it in perspective, my ride to the hospital in the ambulance alone would have been thousands of dollars without coverage. On top of that, meals, meds, therapies, a bed. The financial weight of just trying to get help can be too much for many people.

65

Teacher Becomes Student

There was a window looking into the ICU from my unit's outside smoking area. One night was particularly quiet. I sat on a bench and looked at the moon. I glanced into the ICU and saw my guitar student sitting lifeless on a chair. His head hung like a cannonball tied to a rope. Life is so weird sometimes. One day he's trapped on a campus at a foster school with the system pushing him around, and the next, he is trapped in a psych ward at the whim of our health-care system.

In one of my last process groups, I talked to the other patients about advocating for self. That if we didn't, doctors and therapists could walk all over us. I talked about needing to know the medications we were on. During my last appointment with the psychiatrist on staff, I was told that I was, "Too eager." I wish I had asked him what he meant by it. I realized if I hadn't been "with it" I would have gotten walked on. Not only did I have to use my voice, but I would also have to use it repeatedly in order to be heard.

The last morning had finally come, and morning check-in was happening, but I decided to wait in the hall instead. It was around 8:30 in the morning. I could see outside the unit through the nurse's station, and from a distance, I saw one of my most special guardians: Lindsay.

The first stop we had to make was to the discharging department. I received my bracelet. A harsh, seemingly worn-out woman was there.

"You need to make your first payment. Your copay is $260."

This was not true. It was actually $290. She also said my total out-of-pocket fees incorrectly. I asked her if I absolutely needed to make a payment that day. She then told me I didn't have to but it was recommended and that I needed to use a debit card or give a bank routing number. I told her I could only use a credit card, and she said that would be fine.

I found the whole thing to be sad and ridiculous. To ask someone who just got out of the hospital to cough up money is a surefire way to get readmitted. I felt anxious and just wanted to get out of there. I swiped for 260 dollars and was on my way. When I got to the car, Lindsay had made me a little gift package complete with blue Gatorade™ and chocolate gas station Zingers™, among other treats. She looked at me and said, "I want to be the one that always picks you up."

I was breathing it all in. Moving fast in a car, watching trees fly by. We got to my house, and it was clean. Lindsay had gone in and made sure the chaos was gone. I opened my fridge and my neighbors had stocked it. A new wave of appreciation came over me. I got through and then some.

Once released, I got to make my own choices and go where I wanted to. It made me think of all the people who don't get choices. People with special needs, children from abusive homes, women in many other countries, even our own. A choice seems like such a little thing until you don't get it.

On a rainy Sunday afternoon, I invited people to debrief at my house to go over "The Plan," at the same house that contained the horrific impact of my break. Everyone piled in fast as I offered donuts and drinks. We chatted for a bit, then got down to business. I looked around my living room. I had former partners, an almost partner, coworkers, music friends, music-fan friends, music therapist friends, pre-bipolar-Veronica friends, and once-fringe now-close friends. Everyone was following along as I read "The Plan." Everyone was invested in my life. I looked at each person to remember that moment.

During the meeting, we went into detail. Me peeing my pants, me screaming at Lindsay. I felt courageous. There was no question unanswered, no rock left unturned.

66

The Plan, Analyzed

Lindsay brought in extra insights that
I felt would be useful in this book.

Notes on "The Plan" from a friend's perspective
By Lindsay

Warning Signs

Excessive talk about positive/negative energy
The Friday before V went to the hospital, we had band practice. She seemed mostly okay, and we practiced as usual, but two things stood out. First, when we were working on a new song, she asked me to change a couple lyrics because they were too negative.

After practice, we walked to get something to eat. Out of nowhere, she accused me of being "really negative lately." Even if that were true, V, on a normal day, doesn't just call people out so bluntly. On a normal day, she might have said, "Are you okay? It seems like you have a lot going on…" or something similar.

Not wanting to hear friends' concerns
Any other day, V will stress to others that she wants to know when friends observe signs of mania because it gives her specifics to work with and helps her adjust accordingly. We made up the whole "cantaloupe" code word for this reason—to take the heaviness out of it if friends were scared to bring it up. When V is tripping into mania, this changes, and she doesn't want to hear about it. She would say things like, "I don't need you to send me that negative energy" or "I just need everyone to send me their positive energy."

Seeking validation through energy healer types
After I let V know I was concerned, she was quick to tell me that our friend did Reiki on her and said, "She was doing great... better than her friends thought." When a manic V knows her friends are concerned, but she doesn't want to believe them, I think she seeks out people who are willing to validate her thoughts/behaviors, such as spiritual friends, energy healers, etc. To the blind eye, V's early mania presents itself as positive, spiritual growth—that gets major validation in this circle of people who applaud deep spiritual connection but may not know how to detect certain nuances.

What to do during the warning signs

Tell V you're concerned
Do it right away. It doesn't have to be a super serious conversation; just mention in passing that you've noticed something seemed a little off. Try to have specific examples because she'll ask for them.

Encourage her to check in with her psychologist or psychiatrist
She sees them regularly, but she might be willing to schedule an appointment to address any concerns that have been brought to her attention.

Compare notes with friends
Check in with other people who interact often with V and share observations with each other.

Be Honest with V
I've learned a lot through trial and error in this area. It may be scary to be upfront with V about the steps you and others are taking to follow "The Plan," but try to be as honest as possible with V about your concerns and your actions. She will start to feel ganged up on, so remind her often that we are all on her side; no one is against her or trying to do anything behind her back. Ask when possible (is it okay if I call…) but tell when necessary (I'm just letting you know I'm going to call…).

Red Flags

Interrupting group conversation and the inability to listen to pop culture references
Sometimes, a manic V will abruptly stop a group of people from having a conversation because she can't handle the subject matter, usually when it's either too loud or related to pop culture references that she deems too negative. This time around, she had to stop a group of friends from talking about the r*pe scene in the movie Room. Last time, she wouldn't allow any music with lyrics. At this point, V is reaching a place where she a) makes connections out of everything and b) identifies as God/Jesus and considers all problems of the world (even fictional ones) her burden to bear.

Observing that a child has been molested or accusing an adult of molesting a child
Not sure why, but this is a very common theme in V's mania.

Distrust of Men
Also, a very common theme. Different than a typical rant about sexism/patriarchy. It's less societal and more about "control."

She will typically single out a man or men in her family as the "bad guy." She also becomes less and less trusting of her psychiatrist (male).

What to Do During the Red Flag Signs
I've never seen V come back down from the red flag stage. It's a waiting game at this point where we need to keep her safe and away from potentially dangerous situations until a) she asks to go to the hospital or b) the situation escalates, and we're forced to take action.

Get Family Involved
Again, be honest with V. "I'm going to call Stephanie and your mom, and here are the reasons why."

Make Sure She is Not Alone
This is the trickiest step of all. I don't think there is a perfect way to do this, but I think we did an okay job being a revolving door of friends…the second one person got kicked out, we sent in someone else to try to be with her. I practically begged V to let me stay the night with her for my own peace of mind.

Compare Notes with Friends
When I stayed with V on the final night, Christine (who had just got kicked out) warned me to not drink water there. Any helpful info like this can make a difference. Work together to swiftly shut down any work-related scenarios, etc.

Acknowledge but don't validate
This is a fine line. V's brain is working overtime. She may tell you certain things as fact or ask questions as she tries to process her thoughts. (I am God, or Am I supposed to die? etc.) Responses should be gentle but based in reality. "I know sometimes when you're manic you think you're God, and you have a lot of thoughts about needing to die. But you're not God, you're Veronica. You function better in the world when you're Veronica."

What to Do During Delusions
If you're with V while she's delusional, you're about to experience some odd behavior. You may be able to convince her to lie down for a while, but she will not sleep, so hopefully, you drank a Red Bull before you got there!

Don't Sweat the Small Stuff
At this point, every act "means" something to V (drinking water, peeing her pants, playing music, etc.). Yes, you can remind her gently that she is Veronica and that she doesn't need to read into everything, but you don't necessarily want to start calling out all her weird behaviors because she'll probably tell you to leave. Ask yourself, "Is she safe?" If the answer is "Yes," all you have to do is keep waiting. The escalating will happen on its own—try to stay as calm as possible until then.

Read Her Disposition
Sometimes, V wears a creepy knowing smile; sometimes, she looks really confused and worried. It is during the knowing smiles that she feels self-assured and probably won't hear you out. It is during the confused and worried moments that you can get through and help calm her down with gentle reminders that she is safe, that she is Veronica, that she doesn't need to die. You can even remind her during these points we are happy to take her to the hospital if, at any point, she doesn't feel safe.

Protect V and Yourself
The second episode, V was so paranoid she asked to be taken to the ER. She was terrified that someone was after her. The third episode, she started lighting things on fire, and it got physical. If she feels like she's in danger, it's time to go to the hospital. If you feel like you're in danger, it's time to call the police, who will probably take her to the hospital.

67

My Progress

Here is my progress or maybe more accurately, this has been my journey thus far:

First episode: In hospital for fifteen days. Twelve months of complete recovery time.

Second episode: In hospital for eleven days, and at least three months of complete recovery time.

Third episode: In hospital for eight days, and three weeks of complete recovery time.

This is my journey. It looks nice and tidy and as if the next break would be even easier in terms of time of recovery. This is not to say that it will be the case. Every person is different. Some people end up having clusters of manic episodes or years and years of nothing.

It took three episodes to realize I had to put continued effort into my mental health. I can put it on cruise control, but that doesn't mean I can stop steering. Bipolar, like many mental illnesses, is a lifetime event.

Well over a decade later, and I still think about some of those folks in the hospital.

Sometimes I wonder how they are all doing. I wonder if they all made it.

The road to recovery would have looked quite different without my three-part recipe of medications, therapy, and support. With just one of the three, my chances decrease. With all three, I can live a life like anyone else. Medication is a buoy in the sea of my brain activity. Therapy is a place where I can just be myself because I'm not worried about being judged. I always know I have a group of people I can call who will come help me. It is easy for me to ask for help now.

68

The Interview I Didn't Get

It happens like this with every new psychiatrist or psychologist I get:

Doctor: And who in your family has bipolar?
Me: No one.
Doctor: No one?

The truth is, when my dad passed away four years ago, we found his antidepressants tucked away in a cabinet. My mom would tell stories of how he would buy several of the same book, go on shopping sprees, and have very big emotions. My dad was larger than life to me, and that stupid little piece of cancer somehow got the best of him. It felt like a David and Goliath moment, losing my father.

I'm kicking myself now for not digging a little deeper with my dad. I often wondered about him having bipolar but was too scared to ask. Why can't we talk about it? Bipolar is commonly passed down and it is so well hidden.

We hide what we think is shameful. Being gay and having bipolar are not those things.

69

Until Next Time

Tragedy brings people together. Trauma can bond people in healthy and unhealthy ways. When people gather around the same source of grief, it can naturally make everyone involved closer and more connected. What a tender place, the harsh climate of trauma.

Two days after my third episode's discharge, I had a solo show. I felt pretty wobbly, but felt I could do it. I had to really ask myself if doing the show would push it. But it had been scheduled before I went to the hospital, and I knew it would be a healing experience, and it was. I looked out at my friends as I sang my heart out—music to the rescue yet again. The show was centered around my break, and I sang the songs I had written while I was in the hospital.

My sister, Stephanie, swooped in for seven days to be with me. We had never really gotten the chance to have that much one-on-one time since we were kids. I'll always remember it. A seemingly "bad" experience allowed an even better experience to surface. I slowly locked into place and continued on my track.

Before I got back to work, I emailed all the families I worked with and let them know what really happened. I had families write back about how they knew someone with mental illness. All I got was support and none of them stopped services. I also told the foster kids I work with and it helped open up discussions about struggles we all face on a day-to-day basis. Teaching my students music is important but the times we share our stories and struggles are the most important. To give a space from someone to be bold enough to say "me too" is a gift.

Two weeks after my discharge, I spoke to a group of middle school students about resilience. I spoke about our biggest weaknesses actually being our greatest strength. One girl told the whole class that she had been abused when she was little. I knew it was possible that at least one person in that room thought, "Me Too" because of her ability to come forth and speak up.

I've realized it is in the struggle, too, that I grow. For me, a surefire way to grow is if I am in a struggle and to know that in the moments where I feel lucid, joyful, in the flow, to capture those moments for a rainy day. And on the days I feel empty, to remember the magic of yesterday—because every season, with every type of storm and sun, will find me. I have seen the edges, and while it can send me to my knees, it can also give me a wild sense of gratitude.

Photos by Kate Frisch

70

Letter to Me

Dear Veronica,

I bet right now you are scared, racing, terrified, or on top of the world. Know that things won't always feel like this. Remember who you are. You are Veronica. You are not Jesus or the one and only God. You aren't chosen to sacrifice your life in order for others to be saved.

Things may be rocky for a while, but things will eventually settle down. Do not push the people close to you away. Remember the love and laughter that fills your home. Remember how safe you are and how safe your home is. Remember, no one is out to get you. No one is poisoning your food. Take care of your body. Nourish it.

Remember how loved and fortunate you are. Don't let your thoughts lead you to guilt. You are loved for a reason. When things start to dip down, don't isolate. Keep moving. There's always sunshine just around the corner for you. You've seen that to be true.

Even though Veronica is writing this letter, Manic Veronica will most likely figure out a way to test the validity of this letter.

You've felt euphoric to tears, paralyzed by fear, overwhelmed, anxious, depressed, determined to end life, apathetic, angry. It has brought you right here in this very moment.

Don't give up on yourself, Veronica. Love yourself. Know that I love you so much.

Love,

Veronica.

Scan the QR code above to access and fill out your own Plan.

Scan the QR code above to access a playlist of Veronica May's original music, inspired by living with Bipolar.

This Plan template can be fit to many different types of needs like OCD, anger management, and other invisible and maybe even visible diagnosis. It was designed with Bipolar in mind but is not limited to it. See if this is a good tool for you.

The Plan (TEMPLATE)

My **CODE WORD** if you think I seem a bit "off" is _____. Using a code word can make it easier and quicker to bring it up. I consent to you using this word if you feel like you need to.

Example: Hey, (name), you seem (code word). Everything good?

Phase 1:
Signs of_____ (mania/depression/anxiety etc.)

Create exhaustive list here:

Phase 2:
Signs of_____ (mania/depression/anxiety etc.)

How to get help

1st step SEE IF I CAN HELP MYSELF

What I personally do to help myself in mania/depression (Example: Take a walk)

Create exhaustive list here:

2nd Step CONTACT PEOPLE FOR HELP (Include name and number for all contacts)

Immediately call 1 of 3 main contacts so I'm not alone in the house:

1. (Name) (Relation to me) (phone number)
2. (Name) (Relation to me) (phone number)
3. (Name) (Relation to me) (phone number)
   - Call Psychiatrist – (Name) (Number)
   - Call Psychologist – (Name) (Number)
   - Call Nurse Practitioner— (Name) (Number)

Other people to call in case no one answers:

(List as many (name) (number) as you need to here)

Phase 3:
What other people can do (Example: Go over The Plan with me)

Create exhaustive list here:

Say these specific things to ease my mind (Example: You don't need to read into anything as a secret message to you)

Create exhaustive list here:

Phase 4:
Hospitalization

1. Name of preferred hospital:

Address:

Phone # to ER: (**Helps to call ahead**)

2. Back up hospital:

Address:

Phone # to ER:

3. Last resort hospital:

Address:

Phone # to ER:

Current Medications:

Phase 5:
Discharge Planning

Places I feel safe where I can stay:

    1. (Name) (Relation) (Address)
    2. (Name) (Relation) (Address)
    3. (Name) (Relation) (Address)

Remember You are not a burden.

What to avoid: (Example: crowded places)

Create an exhaustive list here:

Glossary

Some of these definitions are in my words.

Abilify (aka Aripiprazole)
Aripiprazole is a medication used to manage and treat schizophrenia, mania associated with bipolar I disorder, irritability associated with an autism spectrum disorder, disjunctive therapy in major depressive disorder, and Tourette syndrome. https://www.ncbi.nlm.nih.gov/

Bipolar I
Generally erring on the "high" or "manic" side. One qualifier is being institutionalized at least one time. Must have psychosis such as delusions, paranoia, and sometimes hallucinations. Generally, has more periods of rest in between than bipolar II.

Bipolar II
Erring on the low side while still having hypomania in the highs. More of a persistent mood disorder in day-to-day life. Can also have forms of psychosis in their extreme times but that is not as common.

Cyclothymia/Cyclothymic Disorder
Cyclothymia causes emotional ups and downs, but they're not as extreme as those in bipolar I or II disorder. With cyclothymia,

you experience frequent periods when your mood noticeably shifts up and down from baseline.

Delusion
Believing something that is not based in reality or fact. An example of a delusion that pops up for me is that my psychiatrist is Satan and my psychologist is the highest God. It is common for delusions to have religious themes.

Delusions of Grandeur
Believing you are some sort of powerful figure. Generally, a celebrity. Jesus Christ, The Holy Spirit, God, Michael Jackson reincarnated, and Elsa from "Frozen" have been all of my delusions of grandeur.

Depression
Just as depressing as it sounds. A span of time in which a person can experience deep sorrow. Sometimes that feeling is not linked to a situation or circumstance. Difficulty getting out of bed, apathy, hopelessness, and thoughts of ending life thoughts are hallmarks of depression.

Hallucination
Seeing or hearing things that are not there.

Hypomania
Feeling elevated, productive, attractive, and unstoppable. A lot of powerful figures, like Teddy Roosevelt, who was thought to have bipolar, got a lot done in this state. It's diet mania. No psychotic features occur in hypomania. This is a state in which a person with bipolar can live. A person can fully function in this state. For me, this state doesn't last long. When this happens, I either take the reins and take the wagon back to the stables, or I ride off into the crazy, burning sun I call hypermania.

Hypermania
This is a level above hypomania. This is something people with bipolar I will experience. Excessively shopping (like buying 100 of the same book), reckless, risky, and/or odd behaviors, seeing, hearing, and believing things that are not based in reality, and a free pass into the hospital. And by free, I mean I hope you have good insurance.

Lithium
Extended-release tablets used to treat bipolar disorder (formally known as manic-depressive disorder). They work by stabilizing your mood and behavior so there aren't extreme highs and lows. https://my.clevelandclinic.org

Lucid
Sane. With it. Full deck of cards. No screws loose.

Mania
Excitement manifested by mental and physical hyperactivity, disorganization of behavior, and elevation of mood. A misconception of mania is that it's all about excitement, confidence, creativity, and other very positive feelings. While this can be true, there are other feelings that come out of feeling "up." Sort of like drinking your way out of a pool of espresso. Agitated, scattered, jittery, scared, and more.

Manic Episode
A span of time in which a person is experiencing mania which could include heightened mood, and psychosis for at least a week.

Paranoia
Thinking someone is out to get you in some way. Recording phone conversations, plotting to end you, talking about you, or poisoning your food, are common forms of paranoia.

Psychiatrist
The person who prescribes medication.

Psychologist
Think, "psy-CALL-ogist." The person you call or talk to. The person who helps you heal yourself and lets you process.

Psychosis
When you are in a state of insanity. Delusions, hallucinations, and paranoia usually come to the party. This can be naturally induced or drug induced.

Rapid Cycling
Going back and forth between depression and mania at an accelerated rate. Sometimes a person can cycle in a matter of seconds.

Titrate
Slowly moving toward balance. In terms of medication, psychiatrists will have you start a dose low and introduce it to your body. Then they will increase. If you are coming off of a medication, the psychiatrist will have to slowly lower the dose until it's time to stop taking it.

Vraylar
Also known as Cariprazeen, Vraylar treats schizophrenia and bipolar disorder. It works by balancing the levels of dopamine and serotonin in your brain, substances that help regulate mood, behaviors, and thoughts.
https://my.clevelandclinic.org/health/drugs/20257-cariprazine-capsules

www.ingramcontent.com/pod-product-compliance
Lightning Source LLC
Chambersburg PA
CBHW070612030426
42337CB00020B/3767

HORMONE HEALTH SIMPLIFIED

Simple Swaps to Improve Your Physical, Mental, and Sexual Health

Sara and Ben Jensen

Hormone Health Simplified:
Simple Swaps to Improve Your Physical, Mental, and Sexual Health

Copyright © Sara and Ben Jensen (2025)

All rights reserved. No part of this publication may be reproduced, stored in a retrieval system, or transmitted, in any form or by any means, without the prior written permission of the publisher.

ISBN Paperback: 979-8-89576-136-6
ISBN Hardback: 979-8-89576-069-7

Published by: